Output Measures for Public Library Service to Children

A Manual of Standardized Procedures

Part of the Public Library Development Program

Virginia A. Walter

Association for Library Service to Children

Public Library Association

American Library Association

Chicago and London 1992

Cover designed by Harriett Banner

Text designed by Deborah Doering

Composed by Charles Bozett in Garamond and printed on 50-pound Finch Opaque, a pH-neutral stock, and bound in 10-point C1S by IPC, St. Joseph, Michigan

The paper used in this publication meets the minimum requirements of American National Standard for Information Sciences--Permanence of Paper for Printed Library Materials, ANSI Z39.48-1984 ∞

Library of Congress Cataloging-in-Publication Data

Walter, Virginia A.
       Output measures for public library service to children : a manual of standardized procedures / by Virginia A. Walter
          p.   cm.
       Includes bibliographical references and index.
       ISBN 0-8389-3404-8
       1. Libraries, Children's—Statistical methods—Standards—Handbooks, manuals, etc. 2. Public libraries—Administration—Statistical methods—Standards—Handbooks, manuals, etc. I. Association for Library Service to Children. II. Public Library Association. III. Title
       Z718.1.W35   1992
       027.62'5—dc20   91-44354

96 95 94 93 92   5 4 3 2 1

Contents

PART **3** Other Measurement Techniques   61

Appendix: Blank Forms   71

Index   127

Figures

Acknowledgments

OUTPUT MEASURES FOR PUBLIC LIBRARY SERVICE TO CHILDREN is a management tool that was created through the collaborative efforts of two American Library Association divisions, Association for Library Service to Children (ALSC) and Public Library Association (PLA).

In 1986, the PLA Services to Children Committee became aware that the revision to the *Output Measures for Public Libraries* was not going to include specific measures for children's services. Long and numerous discussions by that committee prompted Mary Somerville, then ALSC President, to approach her PLA counterpart, Susan Goldberg, concerning the formation of an interdivisional committee to identify issues and concerns about output measures for children's services. An interdivisional ALSC/PLA Output Measures for Children's Services Committee was appointed in 1987 and recommended to the ALSC and PLA boards of directors the development of a companion volume to *Output Measures for Public Libraries* that would specifically address the needs of service to children and their care givers, a major market segment within the public library community.

In 1990, the ALSC/PLA Output Measures for Children's Services Committee submitted a grant request to the U.S. Department of Education for a project to develop and field test both quantitative and qualitative evaluative measures for public library services to children age 14 years and under and their care givers. The project was awarded $42,014 by the U.S. Department of Education, Library Research and Demonstration Program. Additional financial and in-kind support totaling $12,600 was provided by ALSC, PLA, and test site library systems. In 1990 the committee hired Virginia Walter to serve as the principal investigator and Nancy Van House as the consultant.

The result of this effort is OUTPUT MEASURES FOR PUBLIC LIBRARY SERVICE TO CHILDREN. It is one more tool in the Public Library Development Program (PLDP) products developed by the Public Library Association to assist public libraries in planning, measurement, and evaluation. This manual builds on the expertise and energy of librarians who saw the need to devise methods of assessing the quality of library service offered in a community. We hope it is a salute to their foresight and innovation.

Many individuals have helped us accomplish our charge:

- A special thank-you to the U.S. Department of Education, Library Research and Demonstration Program. The manual never would have been completed so quickly without such strong financial backing and recognition.
- Thank you to Barbara Immroth for encouraging us to follow through on the DOE grant request process and to be ever optimistic.
- Our eternal gratitude and admiration to Virginia Walter and to Nancy Van House for their ability to conceptualize and put into words our many ideas and, at times, rambling discussions.
- The effectiveness of our committee is a noteworthy example of the wonderful results that can be achieved by the collaboration of two ALA divisions. The talent, experience, and energy of the leaders and members of the Association for Library Service to Children (ALSC) and the Public Library Association (PLA) were essential to the completion of our task. Thank you to Susan Roman, Executive Director of ALSC, and Eleanor J. Rodger, Executive Director of PLA, for their continuous support, encouragement, and counsel as we navigated the bureaucratic waters of ALA. There

were also individuals in both ALSC and PLA who provided us with much-needed counsel, encouragement, and direction. Our sincerest thanks and appreciation to the following leaders in our profession:

Kathleen Balcom   Neel Parikh
Jane Botham   Linda Perkins
Mary Kay Chelton   Jane Robbins
June Garcia   Charles W. Robinson
Susan Goldberg   Mary Somerville
Karen Krueger   Douglas L. Zweizig
Mary Jo Lynch

- Thank you to Bonnie Smothers of ALA Books for easing our way through the ALA publishing procedures and process and to Ruth Schaefer of the Baltimore County Public Library for the expressive photographs.

We would also like to join the principal investigator, Virginia Walter, in thanking the consultant, the test site libraries, manuscript readers, language translators, and project research assistant (listed below) whose excellent suggestions and comments make the manual more relevant and user-friendly.

ALSC/PLA Output Measures for Children's Services Committee

CLARA N. BOHRER, Co-chair
   West Bloomfield (Mich.) Township Public Library
KATHLEEN REIF, Co-chair
   Baltimore County (Md.) Public Library
SALLY BARNETT
   Huntsville-Madison County (Ala.) Public Library
TONI BERNARDI
   Multnomah County (Oreg.) Library
BARBARA DIMICK
   Madison (Wis.) Public Library
SHIRLEY FITZGIBBONS
   School of Library and Information Science Indiana University
ELAINE MEYERS
   Phoenix (Ariz.) Public Library
HELEN MULLEN
   Free Library of Philadelphia (Pa.)

Consultant

Nancy A. Van House, School of Library and Information Studies, University of California, Berkeley

Pretest Sites

County of Los Angeles (Calif.) Public Library
   Berta Barrera
   Cheri Bussert
   Heidi Clark
   Fannie Love
   Penny Markey
   Josie Reyes
Glendora (Calif.) Public Library
   Barbara Omark
   Constance Tiffany
Kern County (Calif.) Library
   Linda Dierck
   Diane Duquette
   Sherry Gomez
   Judith Waters

Field Test Sites

Armstrong (Miss.) Library
   Berry Bateman
Concordia Parish (La.) Library
   Amanda Taylor
Phoenix (Ariz.) Public Library
   Josephine Abrams
   June Garcia
   Elaine Meyers
St. Louis (Mo.) Public Library
   Priscilla Dandridge
   Leslie Edmonds
   Retha Hicks
   Glen Holt
Sno-Isle (Wash.) Library System
   Sunny Strong

Manuscript Readers

Kathleen Balcom, Arlington Heights (Ill.) Memorial Library
Sally Barnett, Huntsville-Madison County (Ala.) Public Library
Berry Bateman, Armstrong (Miss.) Library
Mary Bauer, Prince George's County (Md.) Library
Toni Bernardi, Multnomah County (Oreg.) Library
Clara Bohrer, West Bloomfield (Mich.) Township Library
Jane Botham, Milwaukee (Wis.) Public Library
Mary Kay Chelton, Montgomery County (Md.) Library
Sherry Des Enfants, DeKalb County (Ga.) Public Library
Barbara Dimick, Madison (Wis.) Public Library
Leslie Edmonds, St. Louis (Mo.) Public Library

June Garcia, Phoenix (Ariz.) Public Library

Jane Goodwin, Fairfax County (Va.) Public Library

Patsy Hansel, Williamsburg (Va.) Regional Library

Steven Herb, Dauphin County (Pa.) Library System

Barbara Immroth, Graduate School of Library and Information Science, University of Texas at Austin

Karen Krueger, Janesville (Wis.) Public Library

Mary Jo Lynch, American Library Association Office for Research

Penny Markey, County of Los Angeles (Calif.) Public Library

Elaine Meyers, Phoenix (Ariz.) Public Library

Paula Moore, Arlington Heights (Ill.) Memorial Library

Helen Mullen, Free Library of Philadelphia (Pa.)

Hedra Peterman, Free Library of Philadelphia (Pa.)

Kathleen Reif, Baltimore County (Md.) Public Library

Jane Robbins, School of Library and Information Studies, University of Wisconsin, Madison

Maria Salvadore, District of Columbia (D.C.) Public Library

Mary Somerville, Miami-Dade (Fla.) Public Library System

Nancy Van House, School of Library and Information Studies, University of California, Berkeley

Gretchen Wronka, Hennepin County (Minn.) Public Library

Douglas L. Zweizig, School of Library and Information Studies, University of Wisconsin, Madison

Spanish-Language Translation

Clara Chu, Graduate School of Library and Information Science University of California, Los Angeles

Erick Emiliano Chu

Frank Navarro, Los Angeles (Calif.) Public Library

Research Assistance

Michele Wellck, Graduate School of Library and Information Science, University of California, Los Angeles

CLARA N. BOHRER
KATHLEEN REIF

Introduction

This manual has been designed as a practical guide to quantifying and measuring the results, or outputs, of public library service to children. It will be useful to public library directors, trustees, and Children's Services staff as a guide to thinking about how to evaluate the services that the library provides to children.

If you have already had some experience using PLA's planning process and output measures, this manual will seem very comfortable and familiar. The definitions, procedures, and techniques outlined here are based on the two books already published by the American Library Association: *Planning and Role Setting for Public Libraries* and *Output Measures for Public Libraries,* second edition. This is a companion volume to those two earlier publications. There are many references to the earlier "parent" volumes in this book, but you can use this manual by itself without consulting the other publications. It has been designed to build on the work of *Planning and Role Setting for Public Libraries* and *Output Measures for Public Libraries,* second edition, but also to stand on its own.

The approach taken here is to focus on children, people who are 14 years of age and younger, as a segment of the total service population of any public library. We have tailored the basic output measures to reflect library services to one specific and important segment of the library market, children and their care givers. You will find a mixture of techniques for measuring library use by children, library use for children, and use of children's materials collections. As you use this manual, you will probably think of other ways that the basic measures could be modified to analyze library service to other segments of the library market—young adults, older adults, Spanish-speaking people, and so forth.

One important way in which we have modified the original output measures is by taking into account the seasonal nature of public library services for children. Anyone who has worked in a public library knows that the school year produces very different demands for service from children than the summer months do. You will see that fact reflected in the children's output measures by the recommendation that where a "typical" week is the suggested period for collecting data, you select a "typical" week in summer as well as a "typical" week during the school year and collect data for both weeks, calculating the results according to the formula we provide.

Overview of the Measures

Library Use

- **Children's Library Visits per Child** is the average number of visits to the library by people age 14 and younger per child (14 and younger) in the community served. It measures walk-in use of the library.
- **Building Use by Children** indicates the average number of people 14 and under who are in the library at any particular time. Together with **Children's Library Visits per Child**, this measure shows patterns of use.
- **Furniture/Equipment Use by Children** measures the proportion of time, on average, that a particular type of furniture or equipment, such as preschool seating or computer terminals, is in use by people 14 and under.

Materials Use

These measures reflect the extent to which the library's collection is used.

- **Circulation of Children's Materials per Child** measures the use of children's library materials loaned for use outside the library, relative to the number of people age 14 and under in the service area.
- **In-Library Use of Children's Materials per Child** indicates the use of children's library materials within the library, relative to the number of people age 14 and under in the community served.
- **Turnover Rate of Children's Materials** indicates the intensity of use of the children's collection, relating the circulation of children's materials to the total size of the children's collection.

Materials Availability

These measures, all variants of "fill rates," reflect the degree to which children and their care givers are able to find the materials they want during their visits to the library.

- **Children's Fill Rate** is the percentage of searches for library materials by users age 14 and under and adults acting on behalf of children that are successful.
- **Homework Fill Rate** is the proportion of searches for information and/or library materials for homework use by library users age 14 and under and adults acting on behalf of children that are successful.
- **Picture Book Fill Rate** is the percentage of searches for picture books that are successful.

Information Services

Information services help the client use information resources and provide answers to specific questions. Information services include both reference and readers' advisory services.

- **Children's Information Transactions per Child** is the number of information transactions by library users age 14 and under and adults acting on behalf of children per person age 14 and under in the community served.
- **Children's Information Transaction Completion Rate** is the percentage of information transactions by persons age 14 and under and by adults acting on behalf of children that are completed successfully.

Programming

Library staff provide programs that inform, educate, motivate, and entertain children and their care givers as well as promote library use.

- **Children's Program Attendance per Child** measures annual attendance at children's library programs per person age 14 and under in the community served.

Community Relations

Children's Services staff work actively with schools, child care centers, and other community organizations and agencies that serve children and youth. These measures quantify much of the work that is done in the community.

- **Class Visit Rate** measures visits from school classes to the library relative to the total number of school classes in the community.
- **Child Care Center Contact Rate** is the number of contacts between the library and child care centers relative to the number of child care centers in the community.
- **Annual Number of Community Contacts** is the total number of community contacts made by library staff responsible for service to children during the year.

Field-testing the Output Measures

One of the rewards of being the principal investigator on this project was having the opportunity to test the output measures at different libraries across the country. Working with the ALSC/PLA Output Measures for Children's Services Committee, I tried to select sites that were geographically diverse and that represented the various kinds and sizes of public libraries in the United States. What I discovered, in addition to the needed elements of diversity, was that all of the test libraries shared a commitment to serving children and had supportive administrators and highly competent staff who were responsible for service to children in their agencies.

The California libraries that worked with me in the very beginning stages, when I was still developing and pretesting the data collection forms, were Glendora Public Library, Kern County Public Library (Frazier Park and Kernville libraries as well as the Children's Room at the Beale Memorial Library in Bakersfield), and the County of Los Angeles Public Library (A. C. Bilbrew, Los Nietos, and Valencia libraries).

From the helpful feedback provided at these first sites, I redesigned forms and drafted instructions that were used in the next round of testing at St. Louis Public Library in St. Louis, Missouri (Carpenter and Julia Davis branch libraries); Concordia Parish Library in Vidalia, Louisiana; Armstrong Library in Natchez, Mississippi; Phoenix Public Library (Main Children's Room and Cholla branch); and the Edmonds Public Library in Washington, a member of the Sno-Isle Cooperative Library System. Although a Children's Services specialist coordinated each effort, much of the actual data collection and site implementation were handled by generalists or paraprofessional staff. I visited each site, observing the measurement process, talking to the staff, and sometimes participating in the data collection. Once again, the measures and data collection techniques were refined, and rich insights were added to my understanding of the interpretation and use of the measures.

A first draft of the data collection techniques was reviewed by members of the ALSC/PLA Committee at the PLA Conference in San Diego in March 1991. The participating pretest and field site libraries also had an opportunity to review the first draft of this book. Finally, a wide range of readers, listed in the Acknowledgments, read the first draft of the completed manuscript. After incorporating and integrating the best of everybody's generous suggestions, I wrote the manual that you have in your hands right now. It was a collaborative effort from beginning to end. To reflect the collective nature of the creation of this manual, the first person plural, "we," will be the primary voice. We will also address "you" throughout the book, because we feel that we have gotten to know you as we put this publication together.

How This Book Is Organized

Part 1 is an overview of measurement and evaluation, particularly as they apply to children's services in public libraries. This section shows in some detail how this manual relates to its companion volumes in the Public Library Association's Public Library Development Program. It gives some suggestions for managing the measurement effort in your particular library. There is some basic information about statistics and about methods for sound data collection and analysis. The section closes with some ideas for reporting the results of your measurement effort and following up on what you have learned—ways that you can use your data to improve library services for children in your community.

Part 2 is the nitty-gritty how-to-do-it section that presents each output measure for public library services to children in some detail. You will find a definition of each measure, instructions for collecting the data elements needed for that measure, instructions for calculating the measure itself, examples and forms, suggestions about how to interpret and use the results, and ideas about other possibilities you could try.

Keep in mind as you implement these instructions that we have attempted to standardize definitions and procedures as much as possible, so that the way **Circulation of Children's Materials per Child** is measured in Natchez, Mississippi, conforms to the way it is measured in Edmonds, Washington; Los Angeles, California; and Philadelphia, Pennsylvania. We hope that someday public libraries will agree on some basic definitions so that we can continue to build a national data base of statistics on public library services to children. A good start at achieving this goal was made with the inclusion of five data elements that are specific to library service to children in the *Statistical Report '91* produced by the Public Library Data Service. This will help researchers and practitioners as they try to understand the effects of the work we do with children and as they communicate the results of our efforts to elected officials and other stakeholders in the community.

For example, we have defined children as people who are age 14 and under. We do this because that is the primary way the U.S. Bureau of the Census defines a child; therefore, you can use census reports to identify the number of people under age 14 in your community. The Public Library Data Service also defines children in this way because this is the breakdown for age presented in the *County and City Data Book* published by the U.S. Bureau of the Census, a source that is readily available to most libraries.

You may wonder what to do if our standardized definitions don't match the situation in your own library. For example, in your library, you may have already defined juvenile library users as children age 12 and under or all children through the sixth grade. In using this manual, you have several choices. You can collect the data without making the per capita calculation and present it as a raw number. You can try to find some other way of capturing the number of people who are age 12 and under in your legal population area—through a combination of school enrollment figures and census data, perhaps. Or you can, for the purpose of the measurement process, cooperate with the Young Adult Librarian or other appropriate staff and measure the library users who are age 14 and under with the understanding that this will enable you to present the per capita data even though it doesn't reflect the way you have organized your service program. Some libraries may even want to reorganize their service program to conform with the census data.

Part 3 presents some additional techniques for collecting data that depart from the standardized techniques in Part 2. We feel that focus groups and user surveys will help you gather information that is both more subjective and more specific to your particular situation and will help you understand and interpret the quantitative output measure data.

An appendix includes all the blank forms you will need. You may photocopy them and use them as they are or tailor them to meet your own needs. (Suggestions for modifying many of them, as well as cautions about doing this, are included in Part 2.)

Using This Manual

We suggest that you read the first two sections in Part 1, Measurement, Public Libraries, and Service to Children and Managing the Measurement Process, very carefully before you launch into your own measurement effort. Those two sections will help you make the decisions that will guide the process. If you are going to be the one who supervises and coordinates the process, you will also need to look closely at the next chapters on collecting, analyzing, and using the data. Part 2 of the manual is really a reference guide to the output measures themselves. You need to refer only to those output measures that you are actu-

ally going to implement. As you start to work through the output measures you are interested in using, you will see that they aren't as complicated as they may seem at first. The process is the same in each instance: collect the data, calculate the output measure, and interpret the result.

Some Important Definitions

Because this manual addresses library service to a specific segment of the library's community, there are certain elements of the measurement process that must be clarified at the beginning and kept in mind as you use the manual.

- *Children*—In this manual, children are defined as people who are 14 years of age and under.
- *Care givers and adults acting on behalf of children*—Most of the output measures in this manual ask you to consider children's care givers and/or adults acting on behalf of children as well as the children themselves when you are collecting data. This reflects the reality that adults are often the intermediaries between children and the library. Teachers, baby-sitters, scout leaders, child care providers, and parents are all adults who find books at the library, check them out, and share them with children. Children are the end users in these cases. Therefore, we ask you to count adults acting on behalf of children as well as the children themselves.
- *Per child*—We use the term *per child* in place of the more cumbersome term *per juvenile capita*. Many of the output measures in this manual ask you to calculate the measurement in relation to the CHILDREN'S POPULATION OF LEGAL SERVICE AREA, giving you a "per child" figure. This is parallel to the per capita

usage in *Output Measures for Public Libraries,* second edition.

- *Children's Librarian*—For convenience, we frequently use the job title *Children's Librarian* in this manual. We use the term to refer to the staff member who has primary responsibility for serving children and their care givers.

Implementing Good Intentions

It has become clear to many of us over the past decade that good intentions are not enough when it comes to delivering quality public library service to children. Resources are decreasing and the demands are increasing. Children and their care givers need more information in more formats than they ever have before. They need more guidance and motivation from librarians who specialize in the reading interests and information needs of children.

Children's Librarians have learned that they have to be sophisticated managers in order to provide the resources and services that their constituents need. A whole section of *Competencies for Librarians Serving Children in Public Libraries,* adopted in 1989 by the Association for Library Service to Children, deals with the administrative and management skills that Children's Librarians need to demonstrate. This man-

ual is designed to be a helpful tool for implementing and improving those skills.

Sources for Additional Information

Competencies for Librarians Serving Children in Public Libraries. Chicago: Association for Library Service to Children, American Library Association, 1989.

A standard list of the competencies expected of librarians who provide service for children in public libraries.

McClure, Charles R. et al. *Planning and Role Setting for Public Libraries.* Chicago: American Library Association, 1987.

A basic guide to planning for public libraries.

Statistical Report '91. Chicago: American Library Association, 1991.

The latest in an annual series of statistical data about American public libraries, this edition has a special section on service to children.

Van House, Nancy A. et al. *Output Measures for Public Libraries: A Manual of Standardized Procedures,* 2d ed. Chicago: American Library Association, 1987.

Basic measurement techniques for quantifying the outcome of public library service.

The Measurement Process

This section of the manual is designed to give you an overview of the process you will be using when you implement any of the specific output measures described in detail in Part 2. You should read through the next four sections before making any decisions about implementation. By the time you finish Part 1, you should feel comfortable with the terminology and knowledgeable about the basic principles and techniques involved. You will also have an understanding of the managerial decisions and organizational considerations that are a part of the measurement process in public libraries.

Measurement, Public Libraries, and Service to Children

Measurement serves a number of purposes in libraries, as it does in all organizations. Measurements are used to:

- Indicate current levels of performance.
- Compare current levels of performance with both past and desired future levels.
- Diagnose problem areas.
- Develop goals and objectives.
- Monitor progress toward achievement of the library's mission, goals, and objectives.
- Provide quantitative data for decision making.
- Justify budget requests and resource allocations.

There is a long tradition of measurement in public libraries. Librarians have been keeping track of their circulation statistics and book stock since the early days of public libraries. Relatively new, however, are the effort to standardize data collection techniques in order to make the data comparable across organizational boundaries and over time, and the search for ways to quantify the whole range of outputs of library service.

The Public Library Development Program (PLDP), under the sponsorship of the Public Library Association, has been particularly important in promoting the use of standardized techniques and definitions of data elements. PLDP has adopted the systems approach to measurement, which distinguishes between inputs—resources and raw materials—and outputs—the services delivered by the library. The book budget and the staff of the library are inputs; the circulation, programs, and reference transactions are the outputs.

PLDP has built on the earlier work found in *A Planning Process for Public Libraries* by Vernon Palmour et al. (Chicago: American Library Association, 1980) and *Output Measures for Public Libraries* by Douglas L. Zweizig and Eleanor Jo Rodger (Chicago: American Library Association, 1982). After several years of experience with these tools, the PLA New Standards Task Force decided to revise both of them, expanding and developing the notion of library roles suggested by Lowell Martin, and making the output measures more carefully standardized.

The resulting volumes were *Planning and Role Setting for Public Libraries* by Charles R. McClure et al. (Chicago: American Library Association, 1987) and *Output Measures for Public Libraries,* second edition, by Nancy Van House et al. (Chicago: American Library Association, 1987). In addition, the Public Library Data Service was established to collect and publish comparable data from public libraries throughout the country. It has produced a volume of national statistics annually since 1988. With the 1987 manuals as guides, public librarians have been able to formulate and measure the performance of their library service plans with more reliability and comparability than they could in the past.

Measurement and the Planning Process

Measurement is an integral part of the planning process, and the output measures are designed for use at several of the steps in that process. In *Planning and Role Setting for Public Libraries,* the interrelationships of output measures and phases of the planning process are described as follows:

Looking Around: Various output measures can be used to collect information about the library as part of the needs assessment process.

Roles and Mission: A set of roles or service profiles are described that help libraries define their mission and determine the services they can best provide in their communities. Each role description indicates at least one output measure that may be used to monitor progress toward meeting the objectives of that role

Goals and Objectives: The library drafts measurable objectives for each of its chosen roles. These objectives provide concrete targets for the library to strive toward as it fulfills its mission. Output measures are the building blocks for creating those measurable objectives; they reflect common public library services and practices.

Taking Action: In this step, the library decides what activities it will undertake to meet its objectives. Output measures quantify those activities.

Reviewing Results: By analyzing the output measures data, staff can see how the library is doing toward meeting its objectives and begin to think about whether its roles, mission, goals, objectives, or activities are still relevant and useful to the community.

Of course, you can use the measures in this manual without planning, and you can plan without using the measures. You may use a planning process different from the one PLA has developed. The techniques and approaches described in Part 2 are useful in many areas of management. Just keep in mind that these output measures are most useful when combined with a planning process.

Applying the Planning Process and Output Measures to Library Service to Children

There are eight roles described in *Planning and Role Setting for Public Libraries.* Only one of them, Preschoolers' Door to Learning, specifically targets children. This has led some people in the library community to conclude that children were specifically excluded from the other roles, although this was not at all the intent of the creators of those roles. Any of the roles can be applied to service to children. To show how this works, we can look at each role in turn and show how it might be adapted for children's services. For each role, we will give the general definition as supplied by *Planning and Role Setting for Public Libraries* and show how Children's Services staff might implement the general role.

1. *Community Activities Center:* "The library is a central focus point for community activities, meetings, and services."

   When applied to service for children, this role mandates a focus on individuals, agencies, and organizations who serve children and youth in the community. It usually involves an emphasis on programming. The library might provide meeting space for youth groups, such as Boy Scouts, or even sponsor a group itself. The Children's Librarian would be involved in local organizations with a focus on youth and would encourage them to meet at the library on a regular basis. (This role is particularly important for communities with a scarcity of public meeting space.) The library itself would sponsor a lively schedule of social, cultural, informational, and recreational programs and activities for all ages, including children.

   The library might be involved in cable television, with the Children's Librarian providing or facilitating programs for children and their care givers. Such programs may include author interviews, creative dramatics, children's book reviews, and parenting tips as well as programs on issues of importance in

the community, such as child abuse, summer activities, or roller blade safety.

The critical resources here are a staff with the energy and skills to make effective contacts in the community and organize programs as well as the physical facility of the library itself. Meeting space is a factor to consider. The materials collection is not emphasized.

Output Measures to consider:
   Children's Library Visits per Child
   Building Use by Children
   Children's Program Attendance per Child
      (could be segmented to indicate family programming or programs for adults conducted by Children's Librarian)
   Annual Number of Community Contacts

2. *Community Information Center:* "The library is a clearinghouse for current information on community organizations, issues, and services."

   When applied to service for children, this role also requires that the Children's Librarian be actively involved in community organizations that provide or promote services and programs for children, including parent organizations, coalitions of child care providers, clinics, and social services agencies. If there isn't a local roundtable for youth advocates from a cross section of organizations, the Children's Librarian might want to work with other leaders in the community to start one. The goal is to provide access to a wide range of information relevant to children, their care providers, and other adults interested in the well-being of children in your community.

   The Children's Librarian will work to provide the needed information in a variety of formats—books, electronic data bases, pamphlets, bulletin boards, information and referral files, videotapes, audiocassettes, informative programs. Children's Services staff might want to work with a group of children to establish a local information and referral data base especially for kids, with information about local clubs, child care, classes at the recreation center, performances by children's entertainers, and such special resources as homework hotlines or consumer information.

   This role demands a thorough community analysis to determine the information needs of the community and to uncover nontraditional sources of information. The Children's Librarian needs to be sure that children's information needs are incorporated into the community survey and that publicity about the library's information resources is also targeted to children.

The critical resources for this role are a staff that is skilled in working with community resources, a collection that focuses on community information in many formats, and a facility that permits programming as a way to disseminate information. It may also be desirable to provide access to information through telephone requests and electronic bulletin boards, in which case adequate telephone lines and appropriate technologies should be in place and available to children as well as to adults.

Output Measures to consider:

Children's Library Visits per Child
Children's Program Attendance per Child
(could be segmented to indicate programs for adults conducted by Children's Librarian)
Children's Information Transactions per Child
Children's Information Transaction Completion Rate

3. *Formal Education Support Center:* "The library assists students of all ages in meeting educational objectives established during their formal courses of study."

When applied to service to children, this role assumes that the library is an active partner to the educational institutions serving children in the community. The Children's Librarian will work with the School Library Media Instructor in the neighborhood schools to establish parameters of service. The Children's Librarian will also work with teachers to determine curriculum needs. In addition to visiting classes, Children's Services staff may invite classes to visit the library for bibliographic instruction and use of the collection. Efforts will be made to ensure that the materials collection supports curriculum as well as individual recreational and information needs of children. Some libraries might establish after-school homework centers, with volunteer tutors helping children with school assignments. It may be appropriate to display school textbooks or establish reserve shelves for homework materials.

The critical resources for this role are a materials collection that supports the local school curriculum, staff who are skilled in networking with educators and assisting children

with school-related information needs, and a physical facility with table seating for classroom groups of children.

Output Measures to consider:

Children's Library Visits per Child
Furniture/Equipment Use by Children
In-Library Use of Children's Materials per Child
Homework Fill Rate
Children's Information Transactions per Child
Children's Information Transaction Completion Rate
Class Visit Rate

4. *Independent Learning Center:* "The library supports individuals of all ages pursuing a sustained program of learning independent of any educational provider."

When applied to service to children, this role assumes that children have learning goals and needs that are not met in formal classroom settings. The library that adopts this role might want to provide after-school programs for children that address some of those needs, for example, American Sign Language, baseball card collecting, crafts, computer literacy, Spanish conversation classes, bicycle repair, or roller blade safety. In addition, the Children's Librarian might want to establish a computer-assisted learning center with software that is designed especially for children.

Critical resources for this role include staff (or volunteers) who can provide assistance with various learning activities, a juvenile materials collection that supports a wide range of independent learning, and appropriate technology, including computers and software.

Output Measures to consider:

Children's Library Visits per Child
Furniture/Equipment Use by Children
In-Library Use of Children's Materials per Child
Children's Fill Rate
Children's Program Attendance per Child

5. *Popular Materials Center:* "The library features current, high-demand, high-interest materials in a variety of formats for persons of all ages."

When applied to service to children, this role assumes that the library will provide high-demand, high-interest materials for children as well as for adults. The Children's Librarian would provide materials that reflect popular culture as well as the more traditional "quality" materials found in juvenile collections. Comic books, mass market items featuring currently popular media figures, popular music materials, and videos would be among the materials that the Children's Librarian would consider providing for children. Perennial favorites, such as the Curious George books or titles by Judy Blume, would be bought in multiple copies. Staff would make an effort to market all materials aggressively through promotional and merchandising techniques that appeal to children and their care givers.

The most critical resource for this role is probably the collection itself, with enough duplicate copies of popular items to meet the demands of young library users. Staff must be knowledgeable about current reading and media interests of children, be able to interpret trends and to acquire popular materials in a timely manner, and be able to display and merchandise the materials effectively. It is important to have the capability of acquiring popular current materials and getting them on the shelf quickly. The facility would be designed for browsing, with appealing displays and strong signage; it should be easily accessible to children and their care givers.

Output Measures to consider:

Circulation of Children's Materials per Child
In-Library Use of Children's Materials per Child

Turnover Rate of Children's Materials
Children's Fill Rate

6. *Preschoolers' Door to Learning:* "The library encourages young children to develop an interest in reading and learning through services for children, and for parents and children together."

Planning and Role Setting for Public Libraries has a good discussion of this role, which clearly targets preschool children and their care givers as its primary market. Where this is a formal role for the library, the Children's Librarian will work actively with nursery schools, child care centers, parents, and other care givers to promote learning readiness and emergent literacy in young children. The collection will be strong in parenting and child development materials written for adults as well as the board books, picture books, software, videos, and cassettes that are provided for young children. The library may also provide puppets, educational games, and other realia to support this role. Services would include such programs as family story times, toddler story hours, parenting workshops, and outreach to child care centers.

The critical resources for this role include a collection that meets the needs of preschoolers and their adult care givers, as indicated earlier. It assumes multiple copies of popular titles. The staff is knowledgeable about early childhood development, emergent literacy, and parenting and is effective in guiding children and adults through individual counseling and programs. The facility includes space for family programming and shelving and furnishings that are attractive, comfortable, and safe for young children and families.

Output Measures to consider:

Circulation of Children's Materials per Child (could be segmented to indicate Picture Book Circulation per Preschool Child)
Children's Library Visits per Child (could be segmented to indicate Preschool Library Visits per Preschool Child)
Children's Program Attendance per Child (could be segmented to indicate Preschool Program Attendance per Preschool Child or Family Programming)
Turnover Rate of Children's Materials (Could be segmented to indicate Picture Book Turnover Rate)
Child Care Center Contact Rate

7. *Reference Library*: "The library actively provides timely, accurate, and useful information for community residents."

When applied to service to children, the library should be sure first of all that children have equal access to all information resources, including referrals and online data bases. Although there may be a service point established particularly for children, all library staff would be trained to respond effectively to children's questions. It may also be necessary to train adult reference staff in the use of some of the specialized reference tools available in the children's collection.

The Children's Librarian who is implementing this role would want to be sure that the collection reflected the variety of information needs of children in the community; a good needs assessment targeted at children would help with this. It may be necessary to create special information files and information sources to meet information needs of children that are not met by traditional library sources.

Critical resources for this role include a col-lection that emphasizes informational materials for children in all formats and at all reading levels. Staff is knowledgeable in a variety of subjects, including those of interest to children, and is trained to use all parts of the collection to meet the information needs of young patrons. Staff is skilled in interview techniques with children, helping them to formulate research strategies and to retrieve information. Library policies facilitate children's access to information in all formats. The facility should make its information function clear through signage and visible service points. Remote access should be provided through telephone lines and dial-up electronic modes when appropriate.

Output Measures to consider:

**Children's Information Transactions
    per Child
Children's Information Transaction
    Completion Rate
In-Library Use of Children's Materials
    per Child**

8. *Research Center:* "The library assists scholars and researchers to conduct in-depth studies, investigate specific areas of knowledge, and create new knowledge."

When applied to service to children, it is easiest to imagine this role implemented in a library with an extensive and/or specialized collection of children's library materials. It might be a Children's Literature Department in a central library with extensive historical and contemporary holdings, or it might be a special collection featuring a local author or a particular subject, such as dolls, African-American culture, or award-winning children's books. Any of these special collections would be of interest to scholars and researchers.

It should also be remembered, however, that children themselves are sometimes serious researchers and may require access to the special collections of a research library. Libraries selecting this role should evaluate their policies and remove barriers that would limit legitimate access by children. Local history collections, for example, are often especially valuable sources of information for children doing school reports.

Critical resources for this role include a collection with the depth to support its special areas of strength and staff who are knowledgeable in the targeted subjects. Staff should be skilled in helping children formulate research strategies and facilitating their retrieval of the information they need. The facility should be large enough to handle storage of and access to the collection. Preservation may be a consideration.

Output Measures to consider:

> **Children's Information Transaction Completion Rate**
> **In-Library Use of Children's Materials per Child**

Some Organizational Considerations

As you read through the role descriptions, you may be tempted to choose them all! However, a library will usually narrow its selection during the planning process to one primary role and two secondary roles that best reflect its overall mission.

The Children's Librarian should be an active participant in the planning process and represent the needs of children in all phases. Some of the ways that the Children's Services staff could participate effectively include:

- Recommending that youth advocates or children themselves be included as community representatives in the planning process.
- Advocating that a children's perspective is included in the "looking around" phase. Investigate community resources of interest to children and their care givers, such as playgrounds, arcades, skateboard parks, Boys and Girls Clubs, child care centers, preschools, and after-school programs of all kinds.
- Checking to see that the needs of children and their care givers are reflected in the final selection of mission, roles, goals, and objectives of the library.
- Working with library administrators to see that the children's department is adequately and fairly budgeted to meet those objectives.
- Implementing output measures that monitor progress of the library in meeting those goals for children and their care givers.

It is possible that in some libraries, individual departments may be encouraged to develop their own roles, goals, and objectives. Where this is the case, the Children's Librarian may initiate a planning process aimed specifically at service to children, families, and adults working with children. Children's Services staff should be sure that their roles, goals, and objectives do not conflict with the overall mission of the library, and that they have the support of the administration of the library.

There are some libraries that have not implemented a formal planning process. Goals and objectives may be quite informal and measurement efforts casual or nonexistent. Children's Librarians in this situation who want to develop more formal planning and measurement strategies should consult first with their administrators. Management may decide to follow the initiative of the Children's Services staff and adopt a planning process for the library as a whole. It is important to carefully assess the climate and circumstances in the organization before launching your own major ad hoc planning and measurement strategy—it may turn out to be disruptive and politically unwise.

Many of the measurement techniques suggested in this manual, however, could be used by any Children's Librarian with a minimum level of effort to begin to collect the data that will enable him or her to evaluate services to children, whether or not the rest of the library participates. Using these specialized output measures, Children's Services staff can more effectively justify their budget requests, allocate existing resources, plan services and programs that meet community needs, and evaluate how they're doing.

Managing the Measurement Process

As you start to think about how you want to use this manual to evaluate and plan services to children in your library, you will want to consider a number of factors relating to your own position, the library as an organization, and the community. With that knowledge as background, you will be able to make informed decisions about scheduling, personnel, and the levels of effort the library is able to expend on the measurement effort.

Your Position in the Library

Are you the administrator of the library? The view from the top of the organization is lofty but sometimes lonely. You will know best how to approach the library board and/or City or County Manager with your evaluation plans. In addition, plan to consult with the people who will actually implement the process. Certainly your Children's Services staff should be involved from the early stages of the decision making and planning. Do they think it's a good idea? What problems do they see? Do they support the concept of evaluation, or do they feel threatened by it? Are they nervous that their own performance is being evaluated?

Are you a Children's Librarian, a Children's Services Coordinator, or the person who is responsible for service to children? If so, you may be in the position of having to convince someone else in authority that launching an effort to measure some aspects of service to children is a good idea. You will need to convince your supervisor that the staff time and other resources involved will be well spent. Your strategy for influencing the decision will depend on a number of things, such as your working relationship with your supervisor, your credibility, your track record, the status of children's services in the library, resources available, organizational priorities, and timing.

Are you working in a library with a very small staff? Some of these output measures were field-tested in small libraries in rural Kern County, California, where one library technician ran the entire operation. Staff members found that they were able to manage and that their patrons appreciated having the service evaluated! Staff weren't surprised by the results but found it helpful to have documentation for some of the service patterns they had been observing.

The Library as an Organization

Now things get more complicated. Even the smallest library has current practices, a structure, resources, a culture, and concerns about timing that should be considered before starting to implement output measures for service to children.

Current Practices

Does the library already have in place a system for monitoring or measuring various aspects of its performance? For example, most libraries have some method in place for keeping track of circulation. Many record numbers of reference queries. How do the techniques in this manual fit with those already in place in your library? Will you have to get other staff or departments to change how they do things in order to implement some new procedure? The more changes are required, the more disruptive the measurement process is likely to be. This isn't necessarily bad. Sometimes it's good to make lots of changes all at once, but it does require some judgment about timing and priorities.

Does your library already use some of the techniques from *Output Measures for Public Libraries,* second edition? Can the output measures for services to children be easily added to the current effort? Are you interested in the same measures as the library as a whole?

Structure

The organizational structure itself is an important variable in how you decide to implement output measures for service to children. You will need to think carefully, for example, about how implementing children's output measures will affect other departments. Some measures require cooperation from other departments, such as reference staff. Administrators may also have questions about why one department should be making special efforts to monitor its outputs and not others. (Here small libraries have a definite advantage—there are fewer structural relationships to negotiate.)

Resources

Resources are a critical element in your decision

making. Although the output measures described in this manual vary in the level of effort required to implement them, *all* require some additional commitment of staff time. Some require a considerable effort. Can the library afford to commit staff time and energy to a specialized evaluation effort? Ironically, if your library has just experienced a major budget cut, this may be just the time that you would want to be able to quantify the effects in terms of service outputs, but it may be just the time when you haven't got the staff resources to implement the measurement procedures. (The moral of that story, of course, is to have the procedures in place *before* the budget cuts occur. Then you'll be ready with credible documentation about the probable effects of potential cuts in resources on the services of the library.)

Organizational Culture

Organizational culture is an intangible but important element in planning change. The culture of the organization is the way that its values are communicated to the staff and public. Does the library pride itself on its formal, businesslike approach to management? Or does it have a more folksy, personal, down-to-earth style? Is it a progressive organization that likes to think that it's on the cutting edge of library and management developments? Or is it a conservative organization that cherishes its traditions? Does management seem to encourage competition—or cooperation? Think about the kinds of employee behavior that are rewarded in your organization. Is innovation valued? Service to the public? Cost-cutting efficiency measures? Loyalty? Collegial staff relationships? Understanding the library's culture can be helpful in developing change strategies that will work in that particular environment.

The Community

In addition to systematically considering what's going on in your library, you will want to think about your community. Are there any services that the community would be especially interested in? A recent cutback in school library services might prompt interest in the public library's educational role, for example. Have elected officials questioned Sunday hours or asked that the library add them? Is literacy an issue? Have there been dramatic demographic changes that have changed the pattern of library use? Factors such as these point to possible strategic uses of specific output measures.

Selecting the Output Measures to Implement

You will be relieved to learn that nobody ever intended *any* library to implement all of the output measures in this manual at any one time. Few libraries will even use *most* of these output measures. We have tried, in fact, to include a wide variety of measures so that any public library could find something here that is appropriate for that particular library. So how will you choose which output measures are right for you, your library, and your community?

If your library has participated in the planning and role-setting process and has formally adopted primary and secondary roles, you have a starting point for your deliberations. In the first section of Part 1, under the heading Applying the Planning Process and Output Measures to Library Service to Children, there is a summary of the roles and their relationship to children's services, with a list of output measures to consider for each role. Look at those output measures first and see how they apply to your library.

Other public libraries have formulated missions and objectives without reference to the eight roles defined in PLA's planning and role-setting process. As you read over the roles, however, you may find that some of them capture the essence of your library's mission and objectives. If so, you can determine which of the suggested output measures give the kind of data that would help you monitor progress toward your own objectives.

Many of these output measures have a natural affinity for one another. They are built from the same data elements or look at similar phenomena from different perspectives. If you have decided to adopt the **Children's Information Transaction Completion Rate**, for example, you may decide to calculate **Children's Information Transactions per Child** as well since it is computed from the same data. Perhaps reference service is a primary role for your library; then you may also want to use **Furniture/Equipment Use by Children** to investigate the intensity of use of both the children's and adult reference desks by young people or **Building Use by Children** to identify the hours of peak use for help in scheduling reference staff.

Another approach would be to start with

something easy, requiring a minimal level of effort. If you just want to get your feet wet, to get your library started with output measures, you might want to select an output measure for which you are already collecting the data elements. Then all you have to do is calculate the measure. Or select an output measure for which the data collection would be easy for you to implement; then evaluate the usefulness of the output measure. What difference will it make for you to know this? Will it help you in planning? Will it help you make better decisions about staffing or collection development? Will it help you justify your next budget request? Will it help to illustrate the impact of children's services if it is published in the next annual report or in a press release? Will it make children's services more accountable?

Scheduling

Let's assume that you have now decided that you are going to implement a selected number of output measures. Now you need to make another series of decisions related to scheduling.

Timing

Deciding exactly when to start implementing output measures can be tricky. You may want to time the start of new procedures to coincide with planning or moving into a new building. The arrival of a new key staff person or major changes in the library board may also indicate opportune moments for starting a measurement process. The budget calendar, fiscal year, and school year are other elements to consider.

If your library engages in a general round of measurement, you will need to coordinate the children's output measures with the overall effort. There were different opinions among staff at the various field test libraries about whether it would be better to schedule the children's output measures at the same time as the general effort or at a different time. Some people felt that it would be less disruptive to collect children's data at the same time as the general data collection was going on. Other people felt that they would rather collect the children's data at another time when it could be emphasized. This is something for you to discuss with your own management team.

It may be helpful to think in terms of a measurement cycle. All of these output measures

have an annual cycle. Once you have established your typical weeks for data collection, you can factor them into the rest of your annual calendar.

Selecting "Typical" Weeks to Sample

Note that most of these output measures are designed to reflect the seasonal nature of children's library services. Summer is not the same as the school year in most public libraries, although the advent of year-round schools in some communities is minimizing the difference. Your next decision, therefore, is to select a typical week in summer and a typical week during the school year.

You will want to avoid a week with any unusual events that might cause odd patterns of service or weeks when you can anticipate that usage will be abnormally light or abnormally heavy. For example, a librarian at one of the test sites said that she wouldn't select a week in February because Black History Month places unusual demands on the collection and the reference staff. Weather might be a factor in your community. Obviously, unexpected events can occur even in your typical week. Who can predict an earthquake, a blizzard, or a major breakdown in the air conditioning system, for example? It is probably best to get a lot of input from staff before you make this decision. Consider the first year a trial run in order to see how it goes. Then settle on a regular pattern that you can follow from year to year.

Another decision that you will have to make if you are using more than one data collection procedure is whether to collect all your data during the same typical weeks. Some libraries prefer to accomplish all of their data collecting in one time period, when the staff is focused on that activity. Other libraries feel that too much emphasis on data collection makes the week less typical or that it requires more staff effort than they can afford to spend. They would rather spread the data collection over a longer period of time. So you may need to select more than one pair of typical weeks. Be aware that your data will be more comparable if it is all collected at the same time.

Allow Enough Time to Get Organized

Give yourself enough time to plan and get organized before you launch on your first data collec-

tion effort. You may need to recruit and train volunteers to help. You will want to train the staff who will be implementing the procedures and inform everybody else. You will need to organize forms and supplies. Pretests may take more time than you think. Be generous with your planning and don't rush into implementation.

Personnel Issues

All of the output measures require effort from people, either regular staff or volunteers. Personnel issues and problems are certain to surface. It is important that you confront them directly. In most libraries, implementing output measures at even a minimal level is an added workload. It also represents a change in the status quo, and this always upsets somebody. Recognize this and account for it as you plan your measurement effort.

Good communication will help considerably. Be sure that your supervisor knows what you're doing and supports the project. Keep colleagues informed throughout the process. Get plenty of input from staff at all levels as you make decisions about the selection of output measures and scheduling. Listen carefully to objections and negative comments. If you don't solve problems during the planning stages, they will come back to haunt you later.

Be sure that everybody is clear about what is expected from them. Have at least one staff meeting devoted to training staff and volunteers in the data collection procedures and to answering questions about the process. Be ready to reassure people that there are no right or wrong results from output measures. They need to understand *why* you're collecting the data and how it's going to be used. You want people to be positive about the process without getting a "Sweeps Week" mentality, trying to hike up the numbers artificially. Written instructions are an important backup to your training session. Be sure that a designated output measures coordinator is on hand during the week to answer any unexpected questions that arise. Empower people to solve problems themselves as well.

Level of Effort

Some of these measures require considerably more effort than others. Some measures can be implemented with different levels of effort, depending on your resources and what you want to find out. Reading the directions for each measure will give you a good indication of what is involved. Some general observations can be made about some of the variables that determine levels of effort:

- *Data source.* If you already have the data, your level of effort will be obviously less than if you must conduct a special data collection. The easiest measures use existing data. **Circulation of Children's Materials per Child** is an easy measure for most libraries because they already know their annual juvenile circulation, and they can retrieve children's population data from census records. Other measures require that library staff keep a tally or count of some activities, items, or people. This requires more effort. User surveys require the most work to implement, so the **Children's Fill Rate** probably requires the highest level of effort.
- *Sampling.* Most of these output measures are based on a sample of transactions or items. It is usually easier and more accurate to sample rather than try to count everything because you're likely to make mistakes trying to count everything. The desirable sample size depends on what you need to know and how precise you need to be. (See the discussion on sampling in the next chapter.)
- *Time.* Usually more effort is required for longer periods of data collection. Don't forget to allow time for compiling and analyzing the data as well.
- *Level of data collected.* Libraries with multiple outlets need to decide whether to collect data at the branch level or for the library as a whole.

If you feel that you need more guidance about the level of effort involved in implementing various output measures, there is a helpful table on page 6 of *Output Measures for Public Libraries,* second edition, that compares the level of effort for the measures presented in that volume. Much of that information is applicable to these output measures for children's services. Be aware that simply adding the element of discriminating by age in the tallies adds to the level of effort.

Collecting, Interpreting, and Using the Data

Collecting and Analyzing the Data

This manual is subtitled *A Manual of Standardized Procedures.* Every effort has been made to develop standardized definitions and standardized procedures so that you can achieve valid, reliable, and comparable results. This will enable you to use the results of your measurement effort with some confidence in their validity, to compare your own results over time, and to compare your results with those of other libraries. At the same time, we have tried to allow for some flexibility in the level of effort required and some variability in the data elements in order to account for the different kinds of libraries that will be implementing these measures and the different uses to which they will be put.

Rigor

To be most useful, measurement results must be valid, reliable, and comparable. A valid measurement is one that measures what it is intended to measure. For example, a children's materials holdings count that is based only on the shelf list may not be valid. Often, uncataloged items not included in the shelflist must be added to make this a valid measure.

To be reliable, the same thing must be counted in the same way by everybody doing the counting. In some instances, this is difficult to achieve. For example, in each measure that requires tallying juvenile users, there is an instruction to identify patrons who are age 14 and under. This is not going to be totally reliable because the methods for doing so are subjective. Observers will have to make subjective judgments based on guidelines that you provide. We have tried, however, to make you aware of the difficulties and some ways to minimize them. We are also somewhat reassured by the probability that for every 15-year-old who is counted in error there is likely to be a mature 13-year-old who was overlooked. What you're aiming for here is as much consistency as possible.

Comparability means that the same things must

be measured in the same way each time. This is one reason why we have defined a juvenile library user as someone who is 14 and under, even though we know that not all libraries define children in this way. This is one of the cutoff years used by the U.S. Bureau of the Census, and we need to have a standardized definition that libraries will agree to *for the purpose of implementing output measures* if the results of those output measures are going to be comparable.

If you follow the directions for the output measures carefully and consistently, your results will be as valid, reliable, and comparable as possible. There will still be individual circumstances that will dictate variations in procedures in some libraries. If you make any changes, be sure to record them so that you will at least be consistent in your variations.

Good planning, good communication, and good supervision should ensure that your measurement effort is consistent and rigorous.

Sampling

Many of the output measures involve sampling. Sometimes a period of time is sampled. Instead of being collected all year, data are collected during typical weeks and then projected to an annual figure. For the fill rates, you sample library users. For the CHILDREN'S MATERIALS HOLDINGS estimation, you sample the shelflist. The basic principle is the same in each case: The sample should be *representative* of the whole.

Sample bias is probably the single most serious error that can occur when designing a sample. A biased sample is one that is *not* representative of the whole. If you selected your typical summer week so that it included your Summer Reading Kickoff Event, you would bias the sample. If you gave your Children's Library Survey only to the "regulars" and avoided giving it to patrons that you don't know by sight, you would bias the sample. If you failed to count babies and toddlers in your tally of Children's Library Visits, you would bias the sample. You see the problems.

Sample size is another critical area. When items are being counted, statisticians recommend that you have at least 100 items in the sample in order to achieve minimally acceptable tolerance levels and confidence intervals. You need 400 items in your sample in order to achieve significantly improved tolerance levels and confidence intervals.

The issue is really how accurate you want or need to be. There is always some margin for error when you project from the sample to the larger population. Tolerance and confidence are the two factors that statisticians use to make a precise sample-size determination.

The tolerance level is the percent within which the measure is expected to be accurate. Most social science research establishes a 3 to 5 percent tolerance level; that is, the findings are expected to be accurate, give or take 3 to 5 percentage points.

The confidence interval is the degree to which you are willing to risk that the sample fails to accurately reflect the total population. The usual acceptable confidence interval for social science research is 5 percent, or five chances out of one hundred that the sample will be inaccurate.

If you want to know more, there is a good discussion of some of these sampling issues and techniques in *Output Measures for Public Libraries,* second edition. The literature on these issues is vast, but you do not need to understand all of it to collect useful output measures. As a basic starting point, what you need to know for each measure is that your sample is as representative of the whole as possible and that you have at least 100 items to count.

Interpreting the Results

Let us say that you have made good decisions at the beginning, planned carefully, and managed the measurement process with grace and skill. Now you must interpret the results and do something about them. In the discussion of each output measure, there are some cautions and hints about interpreting that particular measure. However, some general comments are also in order. Keep in mind that for the most part the output measures only tell you "how many" of something in relation to "how many" of something else. They don't tell you "why" or "how" or "so what." You can make some interesting inferences and speculations by looking at the relationships between measures, as we suggest in the discussion for each one, but you are still just talking about quantities of things.

Quantities of things, of course, are precisely what many management analysts are looking for. Over and over again, you are reminded to develop *quantifiable* objectives, so that you can measure your progress toward achieving them. This manual is largely about counting quantities of things and putting them in context for comparison. Measurement enables you to assign real numbers to things.

One of the most significant trends in public management over the past ten years has been the increased demand for accountability. Taxpayers are more militant about wanting to know what they are getting for their money; public officials, in turn, ask administrators to document the effectiveness of their programs. Budget analysts ask for numbers, quantities of things, as justification for resource allocations.

Caution

1. Biggest is not always best. We've tried to indicate in some of the measures where this admonition is particularly relevant. For example, Preschool Story Hour is usually most effective when the audience is relatively small and intimate. High fill rates may indicate an underused collection where a few patrons report high satisfaction because what they want is always on the shelf.

2. The objective being measured is more important than the measurement itself. There is a danger that when you start counting things, the process of counting will become more important than the thing you are counting. Public administration literature is full of cautionary tales about the unintended consequences of linking accountability for performance to quantitative measures. (You probably have stories you can tell about your local police department and quotas for traffic or parking tickets.) You're aware of the controversy in education about testing. Does it make the schools more accountable for students' learning or does it merely make educators "teach the test"?

   Public libraries are bureaucracies, and bureaucracies are notorious for letting the means take precedence over the ends. Bureaucrats get so skilled at following the rules and procedures that they sometimes forget why the rules and procedures are there. Measurement can easily become an end in itself. Don't let this happen to you.

3. Not everything important that happens in a library is accounted for in quantitative output measures. As we get more sophisticated, we may learn how to quantify some of the intangible events and small miracles that occur in public libraries on a daily basis. Until then, you will have to think of some other way to capture those moments when the immigrant mother listens in as a volunteer grandparent reads to her small child in English, when a

boy catches on to the mysteries of the electronic catalog and the Dewey Decimal system and finds the books on sex all by himself, when a two-year-old masters "Eensy Weensy Spider" at Toddler Story Time, or when an African-American child finds a book about a girl just like her. Cherish and remember all of them. Keep a written log and whenever you can, include them as a vivid supplement to all of your quantitative data.

Acting on the Results

Output measures should provide you with data that are helpful in making more informed management decisions. While some specific applications are suggested for each measure, there are some actions that you should take in almost every case.

1. Inform people about the results. Certainly the staff who have been involved in collecting the data should know what the results were, as well as your administration. If the results are particularly surprising or interesting or positive—or negative—it might be a good idea to spread the news more widely. Many libraries

now publish an annual report that includes such data as output measures. A short narrative explaining the significance of the measures might be a good idea. A press release may be in order. Share the results when you address community groups. People will be impressed with your management sense and your effort to be accountable. In addition, they will have a better picture of what is going on at the library.

2. Make decisions and implement them. Surely the results of your measurement effort will suggest some course of action, even if it means doing more of what you're doing now. Take plenty of time to think about the implications of the output measures; involve your staff and other stakeholders in discussing them. Let people know that the steps you're taking are a result of your analysis of the output measures. If nothing ever happens as a result of the output measures, people will lose interest in them.

3. Follow up. Effective measurement is not a one-time activity. Establish a yearly cycle and stick to it. Modify your measurement process only when you change your objectives.

Above all, remember that the measurement process described in this manual is intended to improve public library service to children and their care givers. If we are going to provide children with the library service they need and deserve, we must have good management skills, good political skills, and good evaluation skills.

Sources for Additional Information

Benne, Mae. *Principles of Children's Services in Public Libraries*. Chicago: American Library Association, 1991.

Chapter 2 presents the children's librarian as manager.

Berk, Richard A., and Peter H. Rossi. *Thinking about Program Evaluation*. Newbury Park, Calif. : Sage, 1990.

A good introduction to some of the issues involved in evaluating programs and services.

Bozeman, Barry, and Jeffrey D. Straussman. *Public Management Strategies: Guidelines for Managerial Effectiveness*. San Francisco: Jossey-Bass, 1990.

A good introduction to concepts of strategic management for public sector administrators.

Chelton, Mary K. "Evaluation of Children's Services." *Library Trends* 37 (Winter 1987): 463–84.

A discussion of evaluation issues in the context of children's services.

Curzon, Susan Carol. *Managing Change: A How-to-Do-It Manual for Planning, Implementing, and Evaluating Change in Libraries*. New York: Neal-Schuman, 1989.

A practical guide to organizational change.

Fitzgibbons, Shirley Grinnell. "Accountability of Library Services for Youth: A Planning, Measurement and Evaluation Model." In Charles C. Curran and F. William Summers, eds., *Library Performance, Accountability, and Responsiveness: Essays in Honor of Ernest R. DeProspo*. Norwood, N.J.: Ablex, 1990.

A scholarly presentation of the history and current issues involved in evaluation of youth services.

Ihrig, Alice B. *Decision-Making for Public Libraries*. Hamden, Conn.: Library Professional Publications, 1989.

Intended for trustees, this is a good introduction to the decision-making process for anybody working in public libraries.

Lancaster, F. Wilfrid. *The Measurement and Evaluation of Library Services*. Arlington, Va.: Information Resources Press, 1977.

A basic guide to measurement methods for libraries.

Marketing: A Planned Approach for the Public Library. 24-min. videotape. Chicago: ALA Video/Library Network, 1989.

A basic presentation, with a valuable discussion guide, on how marketing can aid the planning process.

McClure, Charles R., et al. "Output Measures: Myths, Realities, and Prospects." *Public Libraries* 25 (Summer 1986): 49–52.

An introduction to the use of output measures in public libraries.

McClure, Charles R., et al. *Planning and Role Setting for Public Libraries: A Manual of Options and Procedures*. Chicago: American Library Association, 1987.

One of the basic documents of the Public Library Development Program.

"Monitoring the Quality of Local Government Services," *MIS Report* 19 (February 1987).

A special report published by the Management Information Service of the International City Management Association.

Robbins, Jane, et al. *Evaluation Strategies and Techniques for Public Library Children's Services: A Sourcebook*. Madison, Wis.: Univ. of

Wisconsin–Madison, School of Library and Information Studies, 1990.

A useful collection of readings, sample forms, and practical suggestions derived from the Institute on Evaluation Strategies and Techniques for Public Library Children's Services held in 1989.

Rollock, Barbara. *Public Library Services for Children*. Hamden, Conn.: Library Professional Publications, 1988.

The former Children's Services Coordinator for the New York City Public Library puts library services for children in their organizational, political, and social context.

Slonim, Morris. *Sampling in a Nutshell*. New York: Simon and Schuster, 1960.

An oldie but goodie. Still the most practical basic guide to sampling around.

Swisher, Robert, and Charles R. McClure. *Research for Decision-Making*. Chicago: American Library Association, 1984.

Good source for survey and sampling techniques for applied research in libraries.

Van House, Nancy, et al. *Output Measures for Public Libraries: A Manual of Standardized Procedures*. 2d ed. Chicago: American Library Association, 1987.

The general manual that provides the basis for this specialized manual for children's services.

Wholey, Joseph S., and Kathryn E. Newcomer, eds. *Improving Government Performance: Evaluation Strategies for Strengthening Public Agencies and Programs*. San Francisco: Jossey-Bass, 1989.

A collection of readings recommended for people who want to know more about how library output measures fit with current thinking in public administration.

Wilson, Cynthia M. "Output Measures Identify Problems and Solutions for Middle Schoolers." *Public Libraries* 29 (January/February 1990): 19–22.

Tells how the Bethlehem Public Library in Bethlehem, Pennsylvania, used the PLDP Output Measures and a needs assessment to improve service to middle school children.

Zweizig, Douglas L., Joan A. Braune, and Gloria A. Waity. *Output Measures for Children's Services in Wisconsin Public Libraries*. Madison, Wis.: Univ. of Wisconsin–Madison, School of Library and Information Studies, 1989.

The pioneering product of a pilot study conducted in 1985.

The Output Measures

2

In this section of the manual, you will find each of the measures arranged by type of library service.

As with the output measures presented in *Output Measures for Public Libraries,* second edition, the measures are calculated from specific data elements. Throughout the manual, the measures are in bold type and data elements are capitalized. For example, the measure **Children's Library Visits per Child** is calculated by dividing the data element ANNUAL NUMBER OF CHILDREN'S LIBRARY VISITS by the data element CHILDREN'S POPULATION OF LEGAL SERVICE AREA.

You will see the same format for each measure:

- A definition of the measure.
- A brief description of how it is calculated.
- A brief description of how the data are collected.
- An example.
- Instructions for collecting the data.
- Suggestions for interpreting and using the data.
- Pointers and special considerations, if appropriate.
- Ideas for further possibilities.

Part 2 is a reference guide to the measures themselves. For a more considered discussion of the context in which the output measures would be used, read Part 1.

Children's Population of Legal Service Area

The CHILDREN'S POPULATION OF LEGAL SER-VICE AREA is the basic data element that figures in virtually all of the output measures for library services to children. It is used to calculate per capita figures. We use *per child* to indicate per juvenile capita.

The Legal Service Area is the geographical area for which a public library has been established to offer services and from which (or on behalf of which) the library derives income. It may also include any area served under contract for which this library is the primary service provider. The Legal Service Area may be a city, town, county, or parts of one or more of these.

The CHILDREN'S POPULATION OF LEGAL SERVICE AREA is the number of people 14 years old and under who live in the Legal Service Area of a public library. It is sometimes difficult to determine even the general population of the Legal Service Area, much less the children's population. General population data for your Legal Service Area may be available from your state library agency. Other possible sources include:

- State agencies responsible for planning.
- Local planning departments.
- Local school boards and districts.
- *County and City Data Book* (which reports U.S. census data).
- U.S. census reports.
- *Donnelly Demographics,* an online data base.

Many of the output measures are expressed as per capita figures to reflect the local situation in terms that are vivid and accurate. A measure expressed in raw data—ANNUAL CIRCULATION OF CHILDREN'S MATERIALS, for example—doesn't mean much by itself. You can compare it with ANNUAL CIRCULATION OF CHILDREN'S MATERIALS of previous years or with the ANNUAL CIRCULATION OF CHILDREN'S MATERIALS of other branches in a library system or with the ANNUAL CIRCULATION OF CHILDREN'S MATERIALS of libraries with a similar service population. It would not be useful, however, to compare the ANNUAL CIRCULATION OF CHILDREN'S MATERIALS of a small rural library with the ANNUAL CIRCULATION OF CHILDREN'S MATERIALS of a large suburban library.

The per capita adjustment allows you to see how the ANNUAL CIRCULATION OF CHILDREN'S MATERIALS of a particular library relates to the population it serves. This is a particularly useful thing to know. It is a more concrete statistic, enabling someone to immediately understand its significance. A city council member may not be able to conceptualize the meaning of an ANNUAL CIRCULATION OF CHILDREN'S MATERIALS of 10,000. He or she is more likely to see the pertinence of a **Circulation of Children's Materials per Child** of 10, especially when it is pointed out that this means the library circulated 10 children's books for every child in the township last year.

Care Givers and Adults Acting on Behalf of Children

Most of the output measures in this manual ask you to consider children's care givers and/or adults acting on behalf of children when you are collecting data. See the Introduction for a discussion of the rationale for doing this.

Identifying Children Who Are Age 14 and Under

Many of the data collection instructions ask a staff member or volunteer to identify and count library users who are 14 and younger. They will need guidance in doing this. It is usually too obtrusive to just ask, "How old are you?" Here are some suggestions to share with your data collectors:

- Have data collectors look for school identification, such as school uniforms or book covers. Be ready to tell the data collectors what schools children age 14 and younger would be attending in your neighborhood.
- Ask the data collectors to think of 14-year-olds that they know already. This will give clues to typical behavior, dress, and so on.
- Ask a group of 14-year-olds to meet with your staff and share *their* suggestions for identifying their peers.
- Somebody carrying car keys is probably at least 16, no matter how young they look.
- Reassure your data collectors that they shouldn't worry about this too much. It is probable that for every unsophisticated 15-year-old who is counted in error there is a mature 13-year-old who is skipped. It should all come out even in the end.

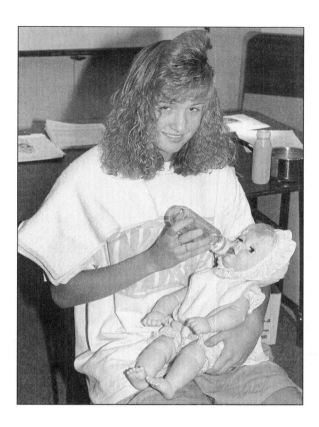

Ask the Young Adult Librarian for more advice about how to identify 14-year-olds in your community.

Libraries with Multiple Outlets

Libraries with branches have special problems when trying to identify the CHILDREN'S POPULATION OF LEGAL SERVICE AREA for each outlet. If your library has already defined Legal Service Areas for each branch, determine whether they conform to census tract boundaries. If so, your job is relatively easy—check the census data for children's population figures.

If the Legal Service Areas have been defined without regard to census tract, you will have to be more creative in determining children's population figures. Check with your local planning jurisdiction to see if anybody else has broken down the population of these areas by age. You can also work with a combination of school enrollment figures and census data. Be sure that the method used for calculating the children's population is consistent for each branch library service area.

If the library has not defined the Legal Service

Area for each of its branches, it will have to do so in order to calculate these output measures and implement the results at a branch level. This can be done by asking the branch librarians to consult a map and informally discuss service boundaries. Or each branch can sample about 200 registration or circulation records and plot the addresses on a map. Service areas can be determined from the resulting patterns. In any case, an administrative decision will be required.

Central libraries present even more difficulties in using per capita measures. If the central library is considered just another branch serving its immediate geographic area, its outputs per capita are very large. If it is treated as if it served the population as a whole, its outputs per capita will be unusually low. If your system has not defined the central library's service area, we recommend that you assume the central library serves the entire population. Just remember what the circumstances are when you analyze and interpret the data.

It may not be possible to collect the data elements that will yield meaningful per capita measures for each branch in a particular multiple outlet library. If that is the case, it is still possible for each outlet to collect data and calculate output measures for the library as a whole.

Library Use Measures

Library Use Measures indicate actual use of the library building and its facilities.

- **Children's Library Visits per Child** is a standard measure adapted from *Output Measures for Public Libraries,* second edition. It indicates the extent to which young library users visit the library for all purposes.
- **Building Use by Children** indicates the average number of people age 14 and under who are in any part of the library at any particular time.
- **Furniture/Equipment Use by Children** is more specialized. It measures the proportion of time, on average, that a particular type of furniture or equipment anywhere within a library, such as public access catalog terminals or seating, is in use by people who are age 14 and younger. We provide a general method for measuring the use of any special facility or equipment; you can adapt it to your own situation easily.

Both the **Building Use by Children** and the **Furniture/Equipment Use by Children** are new to the Public Library Development Program manuals, and we have very little experience in applying them in public libraries across the country. They are adaptations of measures developed for academic libraries in *Measuring Academic Library Performance: A Practical Approach* by Nancy A. Van House, Beth T. Weil, and Charles R.

McClure (Chicago: American Library Association, 1990) and reflect some important early thinking about evaluation of library performance by Ernest DeProspo. We think these measures have considerable potential for giving a richer picture of library use by young people.

Children's Library Visits per Child

Definition:	Number of library visits by people age 14 and under during the year per person age 14 and under in the community served.
Calculation:	ANNUAL NUMBER OF LIBRARY VISITS BY CHILDREN divided by CHILDREN'S POPULATION OF LEGAL SERVICE AREA.
Data Collection:	Count people age 14 and under entering the library building during one week in summer and one week in winter; project for a yearly figure.
Example:	During one sample week in summer, 425 children entered the library. During one sample week during the school year, 530 children entered the library. Multiply 425 × 12 to find the Summer Children's Library Visits; the number is 5100. Multiply 530 × 40 to find the School Year Children's Library Visits; the answer is 21,200. Add the Summer Children's Library Visits (5100) to the School Year Library Visits (21,200) to get the ANNUAL NUMBER OF LIBRARY VISITS BY CHILDREN (26,300). The CHILDREN'S POPULATION OF LEGAL SERVICE AREA is 8533. Divide the ANNUAL NUMBER OF LIBRARY VISITS BY CHILDREN (26,300) by the CHILDREN'S POPULATION OF LEGAL SERVICE AREA (8533) to find the **Children's Library Visits per Child** (3.1). On average, children in this community visited the library 3.1 times during the year.

$$\frac{(425 \times 12) + (530 \times 40)}{8533} = 3.1$$

Collecting the Data

1. Choose a typical week in summer and a typical week during the school year to collect data.
2. Since there is no turnstile on the market yet that is capable of identifying people who are age 14 and under, you will need to use human beings to take this count. It can be quite labor intensive.
3. Decide whether you want to try to count all library users age 14 and under who enter the library during all hours that the library is open or whether you need to sample "typical" hours during the week. Children's library usage is so unpredictable—preschoolers in the morning, after-school rush, families in the evening—that we recommend trying to count during all hours that the library is available to the public.
4. If you can't count for an entire week, the

sample period may be shortened to three mornings, three afternoons, three evenings, one entire Saturday, and one entire Sunday (if the library is open then). Use the Children's Library Visits Sampling Work Sheet (Form 1) to tally your results if you select this sampling approach. Figure 1 shows you a worked example of this form.

5. Some libraries are not open for regular library service during the morning but make their facilities available for scheduled school visits during that time. If this is your practice, be sure to include this factor in your sampling. In other words, if you regularly host visits from schools or other groups during closed hours, be sure that at least one of your sampling periods is a closed period when groups attend.
6. Have someone monitor each entrance to the library and tally people age 14 and under as they enter. Volunteers may be drafted to per-

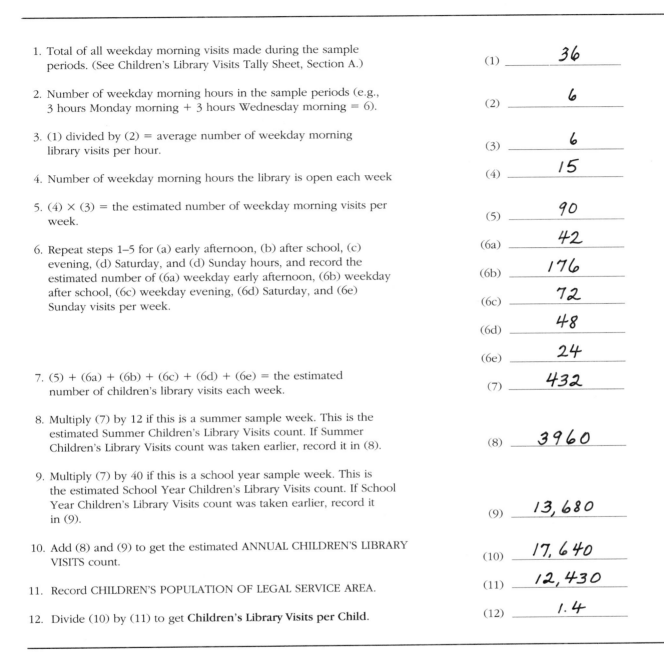

1. Total of all weekday morning visits made during the sample periods. (See Children's Library Visits Tally Sheet, Section A.)

   (1) _____36_____

2. Number of weekday morning hours in the sample periods (e.g., 3 hours Monday morning + 3 hours Wednesday morning = 6).

   (2) _____6_____

3. (1) divided by (2) = average number of weekday morning library visits per hour.

   (3) _____6_____

4. Number of weekday morning hours the library is open each week

   (4) _____15_____

5. (4) × (3) = the estimated number of weekday morning visits per week.

   (5) _____90_____

6. Repeat steps 1–5 for (a) early afternoon, (b) after school, (c) evening, (d) Saturday, and (d) Sunday hours, and record the estimated number of (6a) weekday early afternoon, (6b) weekday after school, (6c) weekday evening, (6d) Saturday, and (6e) Sunday visits per week.

   (6a) _____42_____
   (6b) _____176_____
   (6c) _____72_____
   (6d) _____48_____
   (6e) _____24_____

7. (5) + (6a) + (6b) + (6c) + (6d) + (6e) = the estimated number of children's library visits each week.

   (7) _____432_____

8. Multiply (7) by 12 if this is a summer sample week. This is the estimated Summer Children's Library Visits count. If Summer Children's Library Visits count was taken earlier, record it in (8).

   (8) _____3960_____

9. Multiply (7) by 40 if this is a school year sample week. This is the estimated School Year Children's Library Visits count. If School Year Children's Library Visits count was taken earlier, record it in (9).

   (9) _____13,680_____

10. Add (8) and (9) to get the estimated ANNUAL CHILDREN'S LIBRARY VISITS count.

    (10) _____17,640_____

11. Record CHILDREN'S POPULATION OF LEGAL SERVICE AREA.

    (11) _____12,430_____

12. Divide (10) by (11) to get **Children's Library Visits per Child.**

    (12) _____1.4_____

Figure 1. Worked Example of Form 1: Children's Library Visits Sampling Work Sheet

form this duty during your sample week. It is best if the counters have no other responsibilities during their shift.

7. The person doing the counting may need some guidance on how to distinguish 14-year-olds from 15- or 16-year-olds. See the discussion on Identifying Children Who Are Age 14 and Under at the beginning of Part 2 for some helpful hints.

8. Be sure to count babies and toddlers!

9. Count groups as well as individuals. In other words, if a class of 24 students comes to the library, make 24 hash marks on the form. Some libraries make it a practice to then circle the 24 hash marks to indicate that it was a group; this makes subsequent analysis of the data easier.

10. Use the Children's Library Visits Tally Sheet (Form 2) to keep track of your count. Figure 2 is a worked example of the Children's

Date *Monday, Oct. 21*

Library/Entrance *Main*

Use one tally sheet each day per entrance. Enter number of hours during which data were collected. Count all individuals entering the library who appear to be 14 and younger, *including toddlers and babies.*

A. Morning Visits. Morning is from *10* a.m. to noon, or *2* hours.

Total morning visits *27*

B. Early Afternoon Visits. Early afternoon is from noon to *3* p.m., or *3* hours.

卌 |||

Total early afternoon visits *8*

C. After-School Visits. "After School" is from *3* to *6*, or *3* hours.

卌 卌 卌 卌 卌 卌 卌 卌 ||

Total after-school visits *42*

D. Evening Visits. Evening is from *6* to *9* (closing time) or *3* hours.

卌 卌 卌 卌 |

Total evening visits *21*

TOTAL VISITS THIS DAY *98*

Figure 2. Worked Example of Form 2: Children's Library Visits Tally Sheet

Library Visits Tally Sheet. Some libraries want to know how usage varies by hour; they could design a more detailed form. All that is needed for the output measure, however, is a daily count if you are counting during all available hours.

11. At the end of the sample week, simply count all visits or complete the Children's Library

Visits Sampling Work Sheet. Calculate the appropriate measure—School Year Children's Library Visits count (number of visits multiplied by 40) or Summer Children's Library Visits count (number of visits multiplied by 12). Add the two counts together to find the ANNUAL NUMBER OF LIBRARY VISITS BY CHILDREN. Divide the ANNUAL NUMBER OF LIBRARY VISITS BY CHILDREN by the CHILDREN'S POPULATION OF LEGAL SERVICE AREA to get the **Children's Library Visits per Child** measure.

Interpreting and Using the Data

1. **Children's Library Visits per Child** relates the number of people who are 14 and under who visit the library to the total number of people who are 14 and under in your service area. It doesn't try to explain *why* they visit the library.
2. If you want to increase **Children's Library Visits per Child**, you could:

   • Modify hours to better meet needs of children and families in your community.
   • Publicize the library more to your target population.
   • Offer programs that will attract children and/or families.
   • Evaluate your materials collection to see if it is meeting the needs of children in your community.
   • Evaluate the environmental conditions around the library as they affect children in your community:

     Are there secure and easy-to-use bike racks?
     Is there adequate parking for parents who drive their children to the library?
     Is traffic a problem for children who walk or ride bikes?
     Is the neighborhood safe for children?

   > Note that environmental problems such as these usually cannot be solved by one individual. They may require administrative support and united action by many interested people. You may want to organize a coalition of neighborhood people to work on these issues.

3. A close look at the pattern of juvenile library visits may help you determine appropriate staffing levels. You may need additional staff at the children's service desk after school, or you may be surprised to see how many children use the library in the morning. Comparison of summer and school year patterns of use may also give you useful management information.

Further Possibilities

1. If you are particularly interested in after-school use, you might want to isolate the number of visits by people 14 and under from 3:00 to 5:00 and compare it with other time periods. You could also relate this count to one of the facilities use measures in this section, showing the depth of library use by young people at particular times of the day.
2. It may be useful to relate the ANNUAL CIRCULATION OF CHILDREN'S MATERIALS to the ANNUAL NUMBER OF LIBRARY VISITS BY CHILDREN. Divide the ANNUAL CIRCULATION OF CHILDREN'S MATERIALS by the ANNUAL NUMBER OF LIBRARY VISITS BY CHILDREN to determine Circulation of Children's Materials per Children's Library Visit. This number would give you an idea of how many library materials are checked out in relation to actual juvenile library users.
3. You could also relate IN-LIBRARY USE OF CHILDREN'S MATERIALS to the ANNUAL NUMBER OF LIBRARY VISITS BY CHILDREN in the same way.
4. A still more comprehensive picture of juvenile materials usage per juvenile library visit could be obtained by adding ANNUAL CIRCULATION OF CHILDREN'S MATERIALS and IN-LIBRARY USE OF CHILDREN'S MATERIALS and dividing by the ANNUAL NUMBER OF LIBRARY VISITS BY CHILDREN to calculate the Average Children's Materials Use per Children's Library Visit.
5. Compare **Children's Library Visits per Child** with the total Library Visits per Capita, if your library collects that figure. (If there is a turnstile, you probably have an automatic count of the total library visits.)
6. If the data are available, you might want to compare the ANNUAL NUMBER OF LIBRARY VISITS WITH CHILDREN with the number of young people using the parks or museums in your community. If these data are not currently available, you might want to work with other youth advocates to see that other agencies begin to collect this kind of data about their young users.

Building Use by Children

Definition:	Average number of people age 14 and under in any part of the library at any one time.
Calculation:	Calculate averages from sample tallies of numbers of people age 14 and under in the library.
Data Collection:	At selected sample times, count number of people age 14 and under in all parts of the library.
Example:	During a typical week in summer, library staff counted patrons age 14 and younger in all parts of the building at the beginning of each of the 35 hours that the library was open. The total number of young patrons was 233. They divided this total by 35 to find the average, the Summer Building Use by Children (6.6). In a typical week during the school year, the total number of patrons age 14 and under (counted at the beginning of each of the 35 hours that the library was open) was 375. To find the School Year Building Use by Children, divide 375 by 35; the answer is 10.7. To calculate the annual **Building Use by Children**, weight the two averages to account for the school year, which is three times longer than summer. Multiply School Year Building Use by Children (10.7) by 3; the result is 32.1. Add 32.1 and 6.6 (the Summer Building Use by Children); the total is 38.7. Divide 38.7 by 4 to calculate the annual **Building Use by Children** (9.7). On average, there are 9.7 children in the library at any particular time.

$$\frac{233}{35} = 6.6 \quad \frac{375}{35} = 10.7 \quad \frac{6.6 + (10.7 \times 3)}{4} = 9.7$$

Collecting the Data

1. Decide on the sample week or weeks in which you want to take this measure. **Building Use by Children** will vary considerably between the school year and the summer months. If you want an annual **Building Use by Children**, be sure that you sample during both the school year and the summer, as in the example above. In any case, select a typical week or weeks to collect your data.

2. Divide your library into convenient areas or spaces for counting purposes. Some possibilities include the children's reading room, children's stacks, picture book corner, adult reading room, and adult stacks. Be sure that you account for all areas. Write these areas in the "Spaces" column of the Building Use by Children Data Collection Form (Form 3). Figure 3 is a worked example of the form.

3. Determine the times at which you will be taking the count. You may want hour-by-hour totals. If you are trying to project an annual **Building Use by Children**, be sure that you include hours that are representative of all hours that the building is in use, that is, morning, early afternoon, late afternoon, and evening. Write the times that the tally will be taken in the spaces marked "Time" on the Building Use by Children Data Collection Form.

4. At the designated time, a staff member walks through the library and counts all people age 14 and under in each of the spaces listed on the form. You may need to provide guidance in how to distinguish between a 14-year-old and a 15- or 16-year-old. Enter the number of juvenile users in the appropriate cells on the Building Use by Children Data Collection Form.

Calculating the Measure

1. Add the total number of children who were counted at all observation times.

2. Divide the total number of children by the total number of observation times to find the average **Building Use by Children** for the sample period.

3. To find an annual **Building Use by Children** based on summer and school year sample weeks, collect data during a typical summer

Library: *Dewey*

Date: *Mon., Oct. 21*

Directions: At sampling time, go quickly through the library and count the number of people age 14 and younger in each of the following spaces.

Spaces	Users										
	Time: 11 AM	Time: 12	Time: 1 PM	Time: 2 PM	Time: 3 PM	Time: 4 PM	Time: 5 PM	Time: 6 PM	Time: 7 PM	Time: 8 PM	Time:
Children's room	3	0	1	2	8	10	5	3	4	2	
Circulation desk	1	1	1	0	3	2	3	2	3	2	
YA corner	0	0	0	0	1	4	3	1	4	5	
Adult reference	0	0	0	0	1	2	1	1	2	3	
Adult stacks	1	0	1	2	2	4	2	0	3	5	
Adult reading room	0	0	0	1	3	3	3	1	4	4	
Total	5	1	3	5	18	25	17	8	20	21	

Figure 3. Worked Example of Form 3: Building Use by Children Data Collection Form

week and a typical school year week. Calculate Summer Building Use by Children and School Year Building Use by Children as described in steps 1 and 2. Because the school year is three times longer than the summer, the School Year Building Use by Children needs to be weighted three times as much as the Summer Building Use in calculating an annual rate. To do this, multiply the School Year Building Use by 3 to get the weighted School Year Building Use. Add the weighted School Year Building Use and the Summer Building Use and divide by 4 to calculate the **Building Use by Children.**

Using and Interpreting the Data

1. **Building Use by Children** helps you understand the patterns of use of the library building by children. Used with the **Children's Library Visits per Child,** it helps give a picture of the intensity of library use. A high overall **Building Use by Children** indicates a library that is bustling with young users. If a high **Building Use by Children** is combined with a relatively low **Children's Library Visits per Child,** it may indicate that the building is just too small to handle any more business.
2. Analysis of the difference in **Building Use by Children** at different times of the day or at different times of the year may give quantitative support to staffing decisions.

Further Possibilities

1. It may be more useful to know children's use of particular areas or spaces in the building, such as Children's Use of the Adult Reading Room, or Children's Use of the Homework Center.
2. You may want to count *all* users, adults and children, of specific parts of the library, such as the children's reading room or the picture book area.
3. Calculate **Building Use by Children** at particular times to indicate patterns of use. For example, you could calculate After-School Building Use by Children.

Furniture/Equipment Use by Children

Definition:	The proportion of time, on average, that a particular type of furniture or equipment anywhere in the library is being used by a person who is age 14 and younger.
Calculation:	Divide the number of items of furniture or equipment in question that are in use by people age 14 and younger by the number of items available.
Data Collection:	Count total number of items of particular furniture or equipment. Tally number in use by people 14 and under at designated time periods. Tallies are taken during two sample periods during the year, one week in summer and one during the school year, and are generalized for an annual **Furniture/Equipment Use by Children**.
Example:	There are 4 public access computers in the library. The library is open 35 hours a week. During a typical week in summer, staff counted people age 14 and under who were using the computers at the beginning of each of the 35 hours and calculated the use rate for each of the 35 observations by dividing the child users at each time by the number of available computers. To calculate the Summer Computer Use by Children, which is an average, total the 35 individual use rates and divide by 35. The result for this library was .43, or 43 percent. During a typical week during the school year, staff repeated the same data collection and calculation procedures. The School Year Computer Use by Children was .35, or 35 percent. To calculate the annual **Computer Use by Children**, multiply the School Year Computer Use by 3, add the Summer Computer Use by Children, and divide by 4. The **Computer Use by Children** is .37, or 37 percent. There is a 37 percent chance that a computer in the library is being used by a child at any particular time.

$$.35 \times 3 = 1.05 \quad 1.05 + .43 = 1.48 \quad \frac{1.48}{4} = .37$$

Note that the use rate of any furniture or equipment can be calculated. The example is a calculation of the use rate by children of public access computers. Other furniture or equipment that may be of interest includes online catalog terminals, copy machines, seating, and study carrels.

Collecting the Data

1. Decide on the sample week or weeks in which you want to take this measure. Use rates of most juvenile facilities will vary considerably between the school year and the summer months. If you want an annual use rate, be sure that you sample during both the school year and the summer, as in the preceding example. In any case, select a typical week or weeks to collect your data.

2. Decide what facilities you are interested in for this measure. It is not necessary to calculate use rates for *all* facilities, only those accessible to users and those that are meaningful to you. List the facilities to be considered on the Furniture/Equipment Use by Children Data Collection Form (Form 4). Figure 4 is a worked example of the form.

3. Count the total number of each of the facilities available for each type of facility being considered. Record in the "Number Available" column.

Location or Department: _Children's Room_

Directions: At sampling time, go quickly through the library and count the number of people age 14 and younger using each of the following:

Use Rate is Number in Use by persons 14 and under divided by Number Available.

Furniture/Equipment	Number Available	OBSERVATIONS											
		Time:		Time:		Time:		Time:		Time:		Time:	
		# in Use	Use Rate	# in Use	Use Rate	# in Use	Use Rate	# in Use	Use Rate	# in Use	Use Rate	# in Use	Use Rate
Computers	2	1	.50	2	1.00	2	1.00	0	0	0	0		
Public Access Catalogs	4	3	.75	2	.50	2	.50	1	.25	0	0		

Figure 4. Worked Example of Form 4: Furniture/Equipment Use by Children Data Collection Form

4. Decide the times at which the tally will be taken and record these in the "Time" spaces on the form. If you are looking for an overall average use rate, be sure that you include all representative hours that the library is open, that is, morning, early afternoon, late afternoon, evening, and weekend. You may want to calculate these rates separately, to give you an idea about how the use varies throughout the day.

5. At the sampling times, a staff member walks through the library and counts the number of each type of designated facility in use by persons 14 years old and younger. Count facilities, not users. For example, two people using one terminal count as one if one of those users is 14 years old or younger.

6. The person doing the counting may need guidance in determining who is 14 and under. See earlier discussion about identifying 14-year-olds.

Calculating the Measure

1. Divide the number of items of furniture or equipment in use by the total number available to get the **Furniture/Equipment Use by Children** for each observation.

2. To calculate the average **Furniture/Equipment Use by Children,** total the number of individual Use Rates from all copies of the Furniture/Equipment Use by Children Data Collection Form and divide by the number of Use Rates totaled.

3. For an annual **Furniture/Equipment Use by Children,** calculate the Summer Furniture/Equipment Use by Children for a typical week in summer and a School Year Furniture/Equipment Use by Children for a typical week during the school year as described in steps 1 and 2. Weight the School Year Furniture/Equipment Use by Children by multiplying it

by 3. Add the weighted School Year Furniture/Equipment Use by Children to the Summer Furniture/Equipment Use by Children and divide the total by 4 for the annual **Furniture/Equipment Use by Children.**

Interpreting and Using the Data

1. Furniture/Equipment Use Rates indicate the probability that a particular type of furniture or equipment will be in use. If all the designated pieces of furniture or equipment are being used at a given time, the Use Rate is 1.0, or 100 percent. If half of them are in use, the Use Rate is .5, or 50 percent. If three children are waiting to use the public access catalog terminal while one child is using it, the Use Rate is 4.0, or 400 percent.

2. A high Use Rate indicates that a particular facility is well used; a low Use Rate indicates that a facility is less busy. Consistently high rates may mean that a library needs to increase its capacities in that area, for example, add more seating or more terminals. Low Use Rates do not necessarily mean that the library itself is not busy. A library with a high **Circulation of Children's Materials per Child** may have a low Seating Use by Children because library users don't stay in the building to read. On the other hand, a high Seating Use by Children could correlate with a high **Chil-**

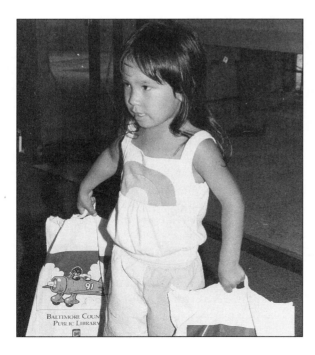

dren's Information Transactions per Child or a high **In-Library Use of Children's Materials per Child.**

3. **Furniture/Equipment Use by Children** calculations can be helpful in doing space planning for building construction or renovation. For example, you may discover that you need more or less juvenile seating than you had anticipated.

Further Possibilities

1. Calculate Adult Use of Children's Furniture/Equipment Rate if you want to know patterns of adult use of particular furniture or equipment in the children's department, such as Adult Use of Juvenile Seating.
2. Calculate Children's Use of Information Desk to help analyze children's use of adult and children's reference desks.
3. Calculate Furniture/Equipment Use by all users and calculate the percentage of those users that are children.

Materials Use Measures

Materials use measures reflect the extent to which the library's collection is used. Three different approaches to measuring materials use are presented here. All three correspond to similar general measures found in *Output Measures for Public Libraries,* second edition.

- **Circulation of Children's Materials per Child** measures the use of children's library materials outside the library, those that are loaned for outside use, relative to the number of people age 14 and under in the service area.
- **In-Library Use of Children's Materials per Child** reflects the use of children's library materials within the library, relative to the children's population.
- **Turnover Rate of Children's Materials** indicates the intensity of the use of the children's collection, relating the circulation of children's materials to the total size of the children's collection.

You need only four data elements to calculate all three measures—ANNUAL CIRCULATION OF CHILDREN'S MATERIALS, ANNUAL IN-LIBRARY USE OF CHILDREN'S MATERIALS, CHILDREN'S POPULATION OF LEGAL SERVICE AREA, and CHILDREN'S MATERIALS HOLDINGS.

Circulation of Children's Materials per Child

Definition:	Average annual circulation of children's materials per person age 14 and under in the community served.
Calculation:	ANNUAL CIRCULATION OF CHILDREN'S MATERIALS divided by CHILDREN'S POPULATION OF LEGAL SERVICE AREA.
Data Collection:	Collected as part of the circulation system by most libraries with automated circulation systems or as a tally in nonautomated libraries.
Example:	A library with a CHILDREN'S POPULATION OF LEGAL SERVICE AREA of 1200 had an ANNUAL CIRCULATION OF CHILDREN'S MATERIALS of 9860, for a **Circulation of Children's Materials per Child** of 8.2. On average, each child in the community checked out 8.2 children's books during the year.

$$\frac{9860}{1200} = 8.2$$

Collecting the Data

1. Note that ANNUAL CIRCULATION OF CHILDREN'S MATERIALS is the total circulation of all children's materials in all formats to all users. It includes renewals. It requires that all children's materials be clearly marked so that the automated system can record them or the circulation staff can easily identify them as juvenile. ANNUAL CIRCULATION OF CHILDREN'S MATERIALS is a count of the juvenile materials that are circulated, no matter who borrows them. It does not aim to measure materials circulated to juvenile borrowers.

2. Most libraries already collect juvenile circulation data as part of their automated circulation system or as a tally in nonautomated systems. If your automated system does not provide this data, you should determine why. It may be that the system can generate the data but that no one has ever asked to have it summarized. If the system cannot currently provide this data, you may want to see if this can be changed; this is basic information that any Children's Librarian and Library Director should have.

3. The usual procedure in nonautomated circulation systems is to simply tally with a hash mark or a click counter every juvenile item that is checked out. This is a notoriously inaccurate method, of course, relying on the staff at the circulation desk to be consistent. Some libraries may prefer to collect this data during sampling periods; if so, be sure that your sampling periods are as typical of children's use patterns as possible.

4. In any case, count all children's materials in all formats that are checked out for use outside the library. Count renewals as circulation. Count interlibrary loan (ILL) transactions when your users check them out to take home; do not include loans made to another library.

5. Calculate the output measure by dividing the ANNUAL CIRCULATION OF CHILDREN'S MATERIALS by the CHILDREN'S POPULATION OF LEGAL SERVICE AREA.

Further Possibilities

1. Calculate the **Circulation of Children's Materials per Child** for particular parts of the collection. For example, you might want to know the Children's Spanish Circulation per Child or the Children's Video Circulation per Child. If you are particularly interested in service to preschoolers, you might want to calculate the Picture Book Circulation per Preschool Child; the census provides population figures for persons under 5.

2. Calculate Circulation of Children's Materials per full-time equivalent staff or per full-time equivalent Children's Librarian for a workload measure or help in staffing analysis.

3. Compare ANNUAL CIRCULATION OF CHILDREN'S MATERIALS to Annual Adult Circulation; compare each to number of professional staff assigned to that service area or to children's and adult library materials budgets.

Interpreting and Using the Data

1. In comparing circulation of children's materials to the number of children in the Legal Service Area, this measure does not take into account juvenile materials borrowed by adults or adult materials borrowed by children. However, it does give an indicator that is consistent and standardized and is probably the best that our statistical methods and data collection techniques can manage right now.

2. A high **Circulation of Children's Materials per Child** indicates heavy use of the circulating collection relative to the number of persons age 14 and under in the community. A library with the role of Popular Materials Center would probably aim for a relatively high count.

3. A high **Circulation of Children's Materials per Child** may also indicate short loan periods, with a resulting high turnover of materials and/or more renewals.

4. A low **Circulation of Children's Materials per Child** may indicate that the children's collection and/or the library hours fail to meet the community's needs. It could also reflect a library with low visibility in the community. Or it may simply reflect a pattern of in-library usage rather than home loans. In some communities, children are encouraged by their parents to use the materials in the library because they don't want the responsibility for borrowed materials. In other communities, particularly where children rely on the public library for school assignments, young library users make heavy use of the reference collection and the photocopy machine and may not check out as many materials to take home.

5. If you want to increase **Circulation of Children's Materials per Child**, consider these strategies:

   • Encourage library use by nonusers. You could:

   Promote your services more actively.
   Add materials more likely to appeal to current nonusers. Has your community changed? Do you need materials in other languages? Other formats? More picture books to meet the needs of young families? More materials to support school assignments?
   Evaluate other barriers to access by children. Do your hours prevent families from coming to the library in the evening? Do busy and/or unsafe streets deter children from coming to the library on their own? Do you need bike racks?
   Consider other methods of materials delivery, such as deposits in child care centers.
   Target specific groups of nonusers, such as child care providers or children of working parents, and devise ways of meeting their needs and promoting the service you create.
   Reevaluate current policies for fees and fines.

   • Increase use of children's materials by current users. You could:

   Use merchandising techniques to encourage impulse reading.
   Analyze **Children's Fill Rates** for weaknesses in your current collection.
   Reevaluate length of loan periods.
   Add or change service hours to better meet needs of children.
   Provide training for all staff in more effective readers' advisory service for children.

In-Library Use of Children's Materials per Child

Definition:	Number of children's materials used in the library per person age 14 and under in the community served.
Calculation:	ANNUAL IN-LIBRARY USE OF CHILDREN'S MATERIALS divided by CHILDREN'S POPULATION OF LEGAL SERVICE AREA.
Data Collection:	For two weeks in a year (one in summer and one during the school year), ask users not to reshelve. Count all children's materials used.
Example:	During one sample week in summer, 124 children's materials were used in the library. Multiply 124 by 12 to get the Summer In-Library Use of Children's Materials count of 1488. During one sample week during the school year, 175 children's items were used in the library. Multiply 175 by 40 to get the School Year In-Library Use of Children's Materials count of 7000. Add the Summer In-Library Use of Children's Materials (1488) to the School Year In-Library Use of Children's Materials (7000) to get the ANNUAL IN-LIBRARY USE OF CHILDREN'S MATERIALS (8488). The CHILDREN'S POPULATION OF LEGAL SERVICE AREA is 5500. Divide the ANNUAL IN-LIBRARY USE OF CHILDREN'S MATERIALS (8488) by the CHILDREN'S POPULATION OF LEGAL SERVICE AREA (5500) to get the **In-Library Use of Children's Materials per Child** of 1.5. An average of 1.5 children's books were used within the library for each child age 14 and under living in the community.

$$\frac{(124 \times 12) + (175 \times 40)}{5500} = 1.5$$

Collecting the Data

1. Any item that is removed from the shelf (or from its usual location) by staff or public is considered used. All formats of library materials should be included—books, magazines, pamphlets, reference materials, computer software, CD-ROM indexes, cassettes, and so forth. Each physical item counts as one.

2. Choose a typical week in summer and a typical week during the school year to collect data.

3. Make a special effort to ask users not to reshelve children's materials during this period. It's a good idea to post signs throughout the library: "Survey in progress. Please do not reshelve materials." Make it easy for people to follow your directions. You might place book trucks or boxes or laundry baskets throughout the library with big signs on them: "Please don't reshelve materials. Leave them here." Frequent verbal reminders are also a good idea, especially with preschoolers.

4. At designated times throughout the day during the sample weeks, collect and count children's materials left on tables, on the floor, on tops of shelves, and/or at collection points. Other Children's Librarians have found that collecting and counting the materials three times during the day (at about noon, at 5:00, and at closing time) is sufficient. If your library is very busy, you may want to collect and count more often. Be sure that counted materials are removed from tables and collection points and placed elsewhere so that you won't count them twice!

5. Use the In-Library Use of Children's Materials Log (Form 5) to collect the counts; use a separate log sheet for each day. You may want to use separate log sheets for different parts of the library. Figure 5 is a worked example of the form.

6. Enter the times when the counts are made on the Log.

7. The rows of the In-Library Use of Children's Materials Log are labeled by type of material. These are the most common categories that Children's Librarians have used. Use whatever categories make sense in your own library. If you don't need to know this level of detail, ignore the categories and record only the totals at the bottom.

Area: *Children's Room*

Date: *Oct. 21*

Use one tally sheet each day. Enter times at the top of the form. At each time listed on the log, collect and count the children's materials left for reshelving on tables, tops of shelves, floor, etc.

Type of Material	Time: 11 AM	Time: 2 PM	Time: 4 PM	Time: 6 PM	Time: 8 PM	TOTAL
Nonfiction	5	3	36	18	20	82
Picture Books	12	15	8	6	19	60
Fiction	0	4	7	9	5	25
Magazines	2	0	8	12	11	33
Sound Recordings	1	2	0	0	4	7
Other *Spanish books*	4	6	2	3	8	23
Other *Software*	3	2	4	5	9	23
Other						
TOTAL	27	32	65	53	76	253

Figure 5. Worked Example of Form 5: In-Library Use of Children's Materials Log

Calculating the Measure

1. If this is a summer week, multiply the overall total by 12 to get the Summer In-Library Use of Children's Materials. If this is a school year week, multiply the overall total by 40 to get the School Year In-Library Use of Children's Materials. Keep a record and add the two totals together to get ANNUAL IN-LIBRARY USE OF CHILDREN'S MATERIALS.
2. Divide the ANNUAL IN-LIBRARY USE OF CHILDREN'S MATERIALS by the CHILDREN'S POPULATION OF LEGAL SERVICE AREA to determine **In-Library Use of Children's Materials per Child**.

Interpreting and Using the Data

1. Adding **In-Library Use of Children's Materials per Child** to juvenile circulation data gives a more complete picture of materials usage than either count alone can give.
2. A high **In-Library Use of Children's Materials per Child** may be associated with a high **Children's Information Transactions per Child**. It

may also indicate a need for relatively more seating in the library or for more copy machines. You may want to use one of the Furniture/Equipment Use Measures to check this.
3. If you want to increase **In-Library Use of Children's Materials per Child**, consider these approaches:

   • Increase seating and study space for children.
   • Evaluate the library's service hours.
   • Make the library more attractive and inviting for children to use.
   • Establish special areas for in-library reading, such as homework centers or family reading nooks.
   • Develop special services for target populations that may find it difficult to check out materials for home use such as homeless families.

4. If you want to decrease **In-Library Use of Children's Materials per Child**, think about these strategies:

- Convert some reference materials to circulating materials.
- Strengthen the circulating collection in areas where the reference collection is currently used heavily. For example, you might want to acquire multiple copies of a good children's encyclopedia for home use.

Further Possibilities

1. Calculate the **In-Library Use of Children's Materials per Child** for particular subject areas or types of materials, such as Chinese-language materials or magazines.
2. Analyze the **In-Library Use of Children's Materials per Child** by time of day.

Turnover Rate of Children's Materials

Definition:	Average circulation per children's volume owned.
Calculation:	ANNUAL CIRCULATION OF CHILDREN'S MATERIALS divided by the library's CHILDREN'S MATERIALS HOLDINGS.
Data Collection:	Use existing data, or estimate collection size by measuring the juvenile shelflist or by measuring children's materials on shelf and adding to number of children's materials in circulation.
Example:	The CHILDREN'S MATERIALS HOLDINGS of a library consist of 5200 cataloged items and 450 uncataloged paperbacks, for a total of 5650 items. The ANNUAL CIRCULATION OF CHILDREN'S MATERIALS is 18,400. Divide the ANNUAL CIRCULATION OF CHILDREN'S MATERIALS (18,400) by the CHILDREN'S MATERIALS HOLDINGS (5650) to get the **Turnover Rate of Children's Materials** (3.3). On average, each item in the children's materials collection was checked out 3.3 times during the year.

$$\frac{18,400}{5650} = 3.3$$

Collecting the Data

1. The ANNUAL CIRCULATION OF CHILDREN'S MATERIALS is the total circulation of all children's materials in all formats to all borrowers for a year.
2. The CHILDREN'S MATERIALS HOLDINGS are the number of cataloged books and other materials plus the number of uncataloged items. Do not count periodicals, whether cataloged or not. Count the actual physical items, not titles. In other words, each copy of *The Cat in the Hat* is counted.
3. Most libraries know what their current holdings are. If you do not have this data, you can make an estimate using one of the following methods:

   - *Physical Inventory.* This is usually appropriate only for small collections. Count juvenile items on the shelves and add to this figure those out in circulation.
   - *Additions and Withdrawals.* If you have a base estimate of your holdings from a previous inventory, update it by subtracting withdrawals and adding new acquisitions.
   - *Automated Records.* Most automated circulation systems have a count of the number of items in the data base. See if it tracks juvenile items.
   - *Measuring the Shelflist.* This works only if you have a comprehensive card shelflist of the juvenile collection. Use Form 6, Children's Materials Holdings Estimation Work Sheet. Figure 6 is a worked example of the work sheet.

     a. Take ten one-inch samples from the juvenile shelflist.

        1) Count the number of drawers in the shelflist and divide by 10. For example, if there are 32 drawers, the result is 3.2. Round down to 3. Take every 3rd drawer until you have ten.
        2) For each drawer, straighten the cards and push them to the front of the drawer. Lay a ruler across the top and

	Cards per inch	Vols. per inch
1. Take ten one-inch samples from the juvenile shelflist.	1a __72__	1b __90__
	2a __68__	2b __82__

For each sample count:
  a) cards per inch
  b) volumes or number
    of copies per inch
	3a __76__	3b __143__

	4a __75__	4b __168__
	5a __71__	5b __135__
	6a __74__	6b __170__
	7a __67__	7b __115__
	8a __72__	8b __300__
	9a __70__	9b __324__
	10a __72__	10b __365__
2. Compute totals of columns (a) and (b).	2c __717__	2d __1892__
3. Divide (2d) by (2c) to get average number of volumes or copies per card.		3 __2.6__
4. Measure the entire shelflist for Total Shelflist Inches.		4 __96"__
5. Divide (2c) by 10 to find Average Number of Cards per Inch.		5 __71.7__
6. Multiply the Average Number of Cards per Inch (5) by the Total Shelflist Inches (4) to get Estimated Number of Cards in Shelflist		6 __6883.2__
7. Multiply the Average Number of Volumes per Card (3) by Estimated Number of Cards in Shelflist (6). Result is Estimated Number of Volumes in Shelflist.		7 __17,896__
8. Enter number of items of children's materials not included in the shelflist.		8 __850__
9. Add (7) + (8) for Total CHILDREN'S MATERIALS HOLDINGS.		9 __18,746__

Figure 6. Worked Example of Form 6: Children's Materials Holdings Estimation Work Sheet

remove a one-inch stack of cards from the middle of the drawer. Repeat until you have ten one-inch stacks from ten different drawers.

b. For each of the one-inch sample stacks, count:

1) The number of cards (line 1, column a, of Form 6).

2) The number of volumes or actual copies represented by the cards in that inch (line 1, column b, of Form 6).

c. Total each of the ten samples to get:

1) Total number of cards per inch (line 2c).

2) Total number of volumes per inch (line 2d).

d. Divide the total number of volumes per inch by the total number of cards per inch to get the average number of volumes or copies per card (line 3).

e. Measure the entire shelflist by compressing the cards in each drawer and using a ruler to measure the number of inches in each drawer. The total for all drawers added together is the total shelflist inches (line 4).

f. Follow the directions on lines 5 through 7 of Form 6, Children's Materials Holdings Estimation Work Sheet, to estimate your cataloged holdings from this information.

g. Add in any materials not included in the shelflist, such as uncataloged paperbacks (line 8).

h. Add line 7 and line 8. The result is an approximation of CHILDREN'S MATERIALS HOLDINGS.

4. To calculate the **Turnover Rate of Children's Materials**, divide the ANNUAL CIRCULATION OF CHILDREN'S MATERIALS by the CHILDREN'S MATERIALS HOLDINGS.

Interpreting and Using the Data

1. Turnover indicates the average number of times that each item in the collection circulates in a chosen period of time. For example, an annual **Turnover Rate of Children's Materials** of 3.3 means that on the average, each children's book, cassette, and other library material circulated more than 3 times during the year.

2. A high **Turnover Rate of Children's Materials** indicates a high circulation compared to the size of the collection.

3. A high-interest, popular collection of circulating materials will tend to have a high turnover rate. Collections with more reference materials or with a broader range of less popular titles will tend to have a lower turnover rate.

4. A high **Turnover Rate of Children's Materials** may result in a low **Children's Fill Rate**; if more items are out in circulation, the less likely it will be that a library user can find what he or she needs at the time.

5. If you want to increase the **Turnover Rate of Children's Materials**, consider these ideas:

- Weed the collection often.
- Buy multiple copies of popular materials and withdraw them when demand wanes.
- Allow as many materials as possible to circulate.
- Use merchandising techniques to call attention to your stock.
- Evaluate service hours, location, suitability of the collection, and other possible barriers to usage. (Most of the strategies for increasing circulation also apply here.)
- Update the shelflist or automated data base of holdings to more accurately reflect withdrawals.

6. If your CHILDREN'S MATERIALS HOLDINGS figures are not accurate, particularly if they do not reflect materials that have been withdrawn or lost, the **Turnover Rate of Children's Materials** will appear to be lower.

Further Possibilities

1. Compute turnover rates for specific types of materials, such as children's videos, children's Spanish-language books, or picture books. This is most feasible where the circulation system is automated, but you could use any of the methods of estimating holdings to calculate holdings in any subject or format if necessary. You should expect that different types of library materials will have different turnover rates.

2. Calculate a turnover rate that accounts for both circulation and in-library use. Add ANNUAL CIRCULATION OF CHILDREN'S MATERIALS and ANNUAL IN-LIBRARY USE OF CHILDREN'S MATERIALS; divide the total by the CHILDREN'S MATERIALS HOLDINGS.

3. Calculate an in-library turnover rate (IN-LIBRARY USE OF CHILDREN'S MATERIALS divided by CHILDREN'S MATERIALS HOLDINGS). You might want to calculate an in-library turnover rate of a non-circulating collection, such as children's software.

4. Calculate turnover rates for specific types of materials during different time periods, such as the turnover rate of children's fiction during summer months or the turnover rate of children's nonfiction during the school year.

Materials Availability Measures

These measures, all variants of Fill Rates, reflect the degree to which library users were able to get the materials they wanted during their visit. Therefore, the measures can give an indication of how well the library's collection meets the needsof its users. The data to calculate these mea-

sures are derived from surveys of library users. We have greatly simplified the survey forms used in *Output Measures for Public Libraries,* second edition, in order to make them easier for young people to fill out. We have sacrificed some of the detail of data, but we think the gain in user friendliness makes it worthwhile.

The basic measure is the **Children's Fill Rate.** For libraries with particular roles, such as Formal Education Support Center or Preschoolers' Door to Learning, we provide specialized fill rates— **Homework Fill Rate** and **Picture Book Fill Rate.** You may think of other fill rates that would be useful in your particular situation; the basic method should apply.

Children's Fill Rate

Definition:	The percentage of successful searches for library materials in any part of the library collection by users age 14 and under and adults acting on behalf of children.
Calculation:	Number of successful searches divided by all searches.
Data Collection:	A survey of library users age 14 and under and adults acting on behalf of users age 14 and under, taken during two sample periods, one in summer and one during the school year.
Example:	During the summer sample period, one library counted 145 items sought by the children and adults who filled out the library survey form. The library counted 112 items found, for a Summer Children's Fill Rate of 77 percent (112 divided by 145). During the school year sample period, the library counted 250 items sought, with a total of 180 found. The School Year Children's Fill Rate is 72 percent (180 divided by 250). To find the annual **Children's Fill Rate,** convert the percentages to decimals. Multiply the School Year Children's Fill Rate by 3. Add the Summer Children's Fill Rate to the weighted School Year Fill Rate, and divide by 4. For this library, the **Children's Fill Rate** is 73 percent. On average, there is a 73 percent chance that a person age 14 and under or an adult acting on behalf of a child has found something he or she wanted in the library during the past year.

$$\frac{112}{145} = .77 \quad \frac{180}{250} = .72 \quad \frac{.77 + (3 \times .72)}{4} = .73$$

Collecting the Data

Scheduling the Survey

1. You must be able to collect and count at least 100 surveys from library users who are 14 and under and adults acting on behalf of children who are 14 and under within a one- or two-week period in order to make valid assumptions about the data. Select typical periods in both summer and the school year to conduct the survey.

2. You will need to decide what days and hours during the sample week you will be handing out the survey forms. You may decide to target *every* child in order to reach the goal of at least 100 completed survey forms. We recommend this method.

   However, staffing considerations may dictate a sample. Then you will want to be sure that you distribute surveys during all times when children and their care givers are likely to be in the library. You will distort the results if you survey only the after-school crowd or if you over-sample the morning hours when parents and preschoolers are in the library. A sampling schedule for a library open Monday and Tuesday from 1:00 to 9:00, Wednesday, Thursday, and Friday from 10:00 to 6:00, and Saturday from 1:00 to 5:00 might be:

Monday: 1:00 to 3:00 and 6:00 to 9:00
Tuesday: 3:00 to 6:00
Wednesday: 10:00 to 12:00 and 3:00 to 6:00
Thursday: 1:00 to 3:00
Friday: 10:00 to 12:00 and 3:00 to 6:00
Saturday: 2:00 to 4:00

Administering the Children's Library Survey

1. One person should be responsible for the survey. This survey coordinator (usually the Children's Librarian) should train all staff and volunteers who will be involved in the survey, gather materials, collect the data, and so forth.
2. Be sure that *all* staff are aware that the survey is taking place and what its purpose is. All staff should be able to answer basic questions from the public and refer appropriate queries to the survey coordinator.
3. Pretesting your procedures is essential; this will help you identify unforeseen problems.
4. Duplicate enough Children's Library Survey forms (Form 7). We have provided a Spanish translation of the form (Form 7a); you may need to have other languages as well. Be sure that your translation is accurate; it is a good idea to have it checked by at least one other person who is fluent in the language. Figure 7 is a worked example of the Children's Library Survey form in English.
5. Number the forms so you will know how many were given out and how many came back. This also helps during tabulation if you need to refer to the original form.
6. Post signs announcing that a survey is being conducted of all library users who are age 14 and under or persons who are acting on behalf of people 14 and under.
7. Place clearly marked collection boxes for completed forms in strategic locations—the circulation desk, children's reference desk, and by the exits.
8. During the sample period, give a form to *every* library user under the age of 14 as well as to adults, such as parents or teachers, who are acting on behalf of children. It

may be difficult to tell if an adult is looking for materials for a child or for his or her own use, even in the children's area of the library. If it is *probable* that the adult is acting on behalf of a child, give the adult a form. The adult can decide not to fill it out if it doesn't apply.

It is not enough to simply have the forms available for people to take. Either a staff member or a volunteer should make contact with each library user. Much of the success of this process depends on how this person approaches the patrons. It can be very empowering for children to be asked for their input. The survey distributor may say something like, "The library wants to know if you are finding what you need here. Please fill this out and help us serve you better." Be assertive and friendly but not overbearing.

Cover all entrances to the library. This fill rate measures the success that children and adults acting on behalf of children have finding materials in any part of the library, not just children's materials.

9. Staff handing out the forms may need guidance in distinguishing patrons who are 14 from those who are 15 or 16. See the discussion on Identifying Children Who Are Age 14 and Under at the beginning of Part 2. You shouldn't worry about this too much, because the form asks how old the patron is. You can discard forms filled out by patrons who are too old. If you have good signage announcing the survey, many people will self-select and offer to fill out the form before you have an opportunity to hand it to them.
10. Although the form is very simple, children under the age of 7 or 8 will need help filling it out. It is all right for a parent, staff member, or volunteer to interview the child and write in the information.
11. Parents and care givers of preschoolers and babies, or other adults acting on behalf of children, should be asked to fill out the survey on behalf of the children. They should give the age of the child, not their own age, and indicate the material sought for the child, not for their own use.
12. If a patron refuses to take a form, the survey distributor should mark it "refused" and drop it in the collection box.
13. Users should fill out the forms just before they leave the library, not as they enter.

Form # __13__

1. How old are you?__10__
   (If you are an adult looking for materials for a child, put down the child's age, not your own.)

2. Were you looking for anything special in the library?   NO

   Please tell us what you were looking for.
   1. _Book about Martin Luther King_____

   Did you find it? (YES) NO   Was it for school? (YES) NO
   2. _Fresh magazine_____

   Did you find it? (YES) NO   Was it for school?   YES (NO)
   3. _Home alone video_____

   Did you find it?   YES (NO)   Was it for school?   YES (NO)

3. If you were just browsing and not looking for anything special, did you find
   anything interesting?   YES   NO

4. Did you come to the library for some completely different reason, such as attending a program
   or using the restroom?   YES

5. Is there anything else you want to tell us about the library? You may write on the
   back of the page if you want to.

   ## GET MORE NEW VIDEOS!!

   Thank you for answering our questions. Please leave this form with the librarian today.

Figure 7. Worked Example of Form 7: Children's Library Survey

Tabulating and Calculating the Data

1. Somebody who is familiar with children's library materials should do the tabulating. Some responses will require an informed eye to determine what was really meant; the tabulator should be able to recognize common children's book titles and frequently requested subjects.

2. Use the Children's Library Survey Log (Form 8). You will need enough copies to record all the survey forms that you distributed. Write the number of each form in the first column. Figure 8 is a worked example.

3. In column (1), enter information drawn from the question "Were you looking for anything special in the library?"

4. Column (2) records information about browsing searches.

5. Column (3) is for recording other uses of the library and forms that were blank or refused.

6. Add up the total for each column and enter on the bottom line of the form. Add the column totals for each page of the log that you have filled out.

7. Turn to the Children's Library Survey Summary (Form 9). Follow the directions to calculate **Children's Fill Rate**. Figure 9 is a worked example. You will also be able to

Form Number	(1) Title, subject, author				(2) Browsing		(3) Other	
	(a) Sought for school		(b) Not for school		(a) Browsers	(b) Found something	(a) Other	(b) Refused, blank, or missing
	(c) Found	(d) Not found	(e) Found	(f) Not found				
1	—	—	2	0	—	—	—	—
2	—	—	1	1	—	—	—	—
3	—	—	—	—	1	1	—	—
4	—	—	1	0	—	—	—	—
5	—	—	3	0	—	—	—	—
6	1	0	—	—	—	—	—	—
7	—	—	—	—	—	—	1	—
8	1	0	—	—	—	—	—	—
9	0	1	—	—	1	1	—	—
10	2	1	1	0	—	—	—	—
11	—	—	—	—	—	—	—	1
12	1	1	1	0	—	—	—	—
13	1	0	1	1	—	—	—	—
14	0	2	—	—	—	—	—	—
15	1	0	1	0	—	—	—	—
16	2	1	—	—	—	—	—	—
17	—	—	—	—	—	—	—	1
TOTAL	9	6	11	2	2	2	1	2
	School items found	School items not found	Nonschool items found	Nonschool items not found	Number of browsers	Browsers finding something	Other	Not usable

Figure 8. Worked Example of Form 8: Children's Library Survey Log

1. Number of questionnaires handed out   225

2. Questionnaires returned with usable title/subject/author or browsing answers (total of questions minus the total of columns 3a and 3b)   182

3. Questionnaires with *only* "other" question checked (total of column 3a)   11

4. Usable questionnaires (subtotal of lines 2 and 3)   193

5. Questionnaires marked "refused," with no usable responses, or never returned (total of 3b)   32

6. Response rate (line 4 divided by line 1)   86%

Children's Fill Rate

7. Title/subject/authors sought (total of columns 1c, d, e, and f)   184

8. Title/subject/authors found (total of columns 1c and 1e)   160

9. Title/subject/authors fill rate (line 8 divided by line 7)   87%

10. Number of browsers (total of column 2a)   34

11. Number of browsers finding something (total of column 2b)   30

12. Browsing fill rate (line 11 divided by line 10)   88%

13. **Children's Fill Rate** (total of line 8 and line 11 divided by total of line 7 and line 10)   87%

Homework Fill Rate

14. Title/subject/authors sought for school (total of column 1c and 1d)   69

15. Title/subject/authors sought for school and found (total of column 1c)   55

16. **Homework Fill Rate** (line 11 divided by line 12)   80%

Figure 9. Worked Example of Form 9: Children's Library Survey Summary

calculate the **Homework Fill Rate** on this form from the data collected if you have used the forms exactly as we have provided them.

Interpreting and Using the Data

1. The fill rates don't tell you *why* any particular patron search is unsuccessful. All they tell you is the probability that a search will be successful. In other words, a 75 percent **Children's Fill Rate** means that a young patron or an adult acting on behalf of a young person age 14 and under has a 75 percent chance of finding something that he or she is looking for.

2. Before trying to interpret what the fill rates mean in your particular situation, it is important to look at them in the context of the library's mission and role and in reference to other output measures. The Materials Use Measures provide some particularly interesting points of reference with fill rates. A very busy library with a high **Circulation of Children's Materials per Child** and/or **Turnover Rate of**

Children's Materials might have a low **Children's Fill Rate** because the collection is so heavily used. Both a library with a large non-circulating collection or an underused library might have high **Children's Fill Rates**.

3. Focus groups might help you understand **Children's Fill Rates** that are particularly high or low. (See discussion of focus groups in Part 3 of this manual.)

4. If you want to increase **Children's Fill Rates**:

   • Reexamine your collection development policy; perhaps you need to add more duplicate copies of popular titles or work harder to determine and meet user needs in your community

   • Make your collection easier to use by arranging it differently or adding better signage.

   • Offer more effective assistance in using the collection. Perhaps the staff needs some additional training in providing readers' advisory service to young library users or perhaps the staff needs to be more visible.

   • Speed up the process of reshelving popular materials.

Further Possibilities

1. As described here, the **Children's Fill Rate** measures access to all library materials by young people under the age of 14 and adults who are acting on behalf of young people. You might want to structure a fill rate that measures access to only children's library materials.

2. The following output measures are examples of ways to customize the **Children's Fill Rate** to provide a specialized fill rate for a particular purpose.

Homework Fill Rate

Definition:	Proportion of searches for information and/or library materials to assist with homework by library users age 14 and under and adults acting on their behalf that are successful.
Calculation:	Number of successful searches for library materials divided by all searches.
Data Collection:	A survey of library users 14 and under and adults acting on behalf of people 14 and under, taken during a sample period.
Example:	During a typical week during the school year, one library found that juvenile library users and their care givers sought 143 items for school use; 95 of those items were found. The **Homework Fill Rate** was calculated to be 66 percent (95 divided by 143). There is a 66 percent chance that a patron age 14 and under or an adult acting on behalf of a child is able to find library materials needed for homework purposes.

$$\frac{95}{143} = .66$$

Collecting the Data and Calculating the Measure

1. See the data collection section for the previous measure, **Children's Fill Rate**. You will probably need to schedule only one sample period, during the school year, for this measure. Otherwise, use the forms and methods described for the more general **Children's Fill Rate**.

2. Calculate the data as indicated on the Children's Library Survey Summary form (Form 9).

Interpreting and Using the Data

1. This measure is particularly meaningful to libraries who have selected the role of Formal Education Support Center. It indicates specifically how successfully the collection supports curriculum needs. A library with a strong educational mission would be looking for relatively high **Homework Fill Rates**.

2. A low **Homework Fill Rate** may be entirely appropriate in a community where school libraries are well developed or where the public library is consciously trying to fill other information and reading needs of its young users.

3. This measure may also give valuable information to libraries who are still looking around, analyzing the community and current patterns of library use.

Picture Book Fill Rate

Definition: The percentage of successful searches for picture books by all library users.

Calculation: Number of successful searches divided by all searches.

Data Collection: A survey of users of the picture book collection, taken during a sample period.

Example: During the sample period, one library counted 225 searches of its picture book collection. Patrons indicated that 195 of those searches were successful. The **Picture Book Fill Rate** is 87 percent (195 divided by 225). There is an 87 percent chance that a patron will be able to find a desired picture book.

$$\frac{195}{225} = .87$$

Collecting the Data

1. Decide whether you want to sample both school year and summer use. If you have any reason to think that school year and summer use vary, you should schedule two sample periods, one during a typical week in summer and one for a typical week during the school year. (See the data collection section for **Children's Fill Rate** for directions for averaging if you decide to use the two sample periods.)

2. You must be able to collect at least 100 surveys from users of your picture book collection during the sample period for the results to be valid. If you are unable to do this in a one- or two-week period, this may not be an appropriate measure for your library to use.

3. We recommend that you survey *every* qualifying library user, that is, every person who looks for a picture book during your sample period. However, if staffing constraints make it impossible to hand out the Picture Book Use Survey form during every hour that the library is open, then you will have to designate particular times during the week that you will target every potential user. Be sure that you designate hours that capture typical users of the collection. A typical sampling schedule for a library open from 10:00 to 9:00 Monday through Thursday, from 10:00 to 6:00 on Friday and Saturday, and from 1:00 to 5:00 on Sunday might be

> Monday, Wednesday, and Friday: 10:00 to 12:00 and 2:00 to 4:00
> Tuesday and Thursday: 3:00 to 5:00 and 7:00 to 9:00
> All day Saturday and Sunday

4. Duplicate enough Picture Book Survey forms (Form 10). We have provided a Spanish translation (Form 10a); you may need other languages as well. Be sure to double-check any translations with one or more fluent readers of the language.

5. Post signs announcing that you are conducting a survey of the use of the picture book collection.

6. Place a box labeled "Completed Picture Book Use Survey Forms" in a conspicuous place in the picture book area. Put another one at the circulation desk and another one at each exit.

7. Number the blank forms. During the sample period, give a Picture Book Use Survey form to each person using the picture book section. A staff member or volunteer must be available to do this at all times during the survey; this person must be able to observe and approach all persons in the picture book area.

8. Adults should be asked to fill in the form on behalf of children in their care who are too young to fill in the form themselves. People who serve as survey distributors should be trained to approach adults in an assertive but friendly way, asking for their help in conducting a survey that will help the library evaluate use of the picture book collection.

9. Unaccompanied children who have difficulty with the form may be "interviewed"; the staff member or volunteer can ask them the questions and fill out the form for them. Children should be approached with respect, asking for the same information. The survey distributor should then say to children who may not be able to fill in the form, "Would you like me to fill in the form for you or would you rather do it yourself?"

10. If a patron refuses to fill in a form, the survey distributor should mark the form "refused" and put it in the collection box.

Tabulating and Calculating the Data

1. Use the Picture Book Survey Log (Form 11). You will need enough copies to record all the survey forms that you handed out. Write the number of each form in the first column.

2. In column 1, enter information drawn from question 2 on the Picture Book Use Survey form. Count the number of items found and not found on each form and enter the totals in the appropriate spaces under columns 1a and 1b.

3. In column 2, record information about browsing searches. In 2a, make a check if the form had either *Yes* or *No* circled for question 3. Check 2b if *Yes* was circled.

4. Make a check in column 3 only if the form was unusable for some reason. If it is unusable, do not mark anything in columns 1 or 2.

5. Add up the total for each column and enter on the bottom line of the form. Add the column totals for each page of the log that you have filled out.

6. Turn to the Picture Book Survey Summary (Form 12). Follow the directions to calculate the **Picture Book Fill Rate**. If you plan to conduct the survey twice during the year, in summer and during the school year, you would follow the directions for the general **Children's Fill Rate** to find the yearly figure.

Interpreting and Using the Data

1. Although this survey measures use of the picture book collection by users of all ages, it would nonetheless be a useful indicator for libraries emphasizing service to preschoolers.

2. Analyze the **Picture Book Fill Rate** in con-

nection with other specialized measures, such as Picture Book Circulation per Preschool Child.

Further Possibilities

1. Use the Picture Book Use Survey forms with parents whose children attend Preschool Story Hour over a period of several weeks or for the time that a particular story hour series lasts. Calculate a **Picture Book Fill Rate** based on just that market segment.
2. Look at the author/title/subject data on individual survey forms to gain a better understanding of specific needs of your picture book users. Use in collection development.

Information Services

Information services help the client use information resources and provide answers to specific questions. In library services to children, information services include both traditional reference work and readers' advisory services, providing guidance on books to read. Two measures apply to reference and readers' advisory services:

- **Children's Information Transactions per Child**
- **Children's Information Transaction Completion Rate**

Both of these measures reflect only those requests to staff for help; they don't reflect questions that patrons answer for themselves without staff assistance.

You may use these measures together or separately. The data collection method described here gathers the data for both measures simultaneously. These measures correspond to Reference Transactions per Capita and Reference Completion Rate as presented in *Output Measures for Public Libraries,* second edition.

A children's information transaction is defined as contact between a library user who is 14 and under or an adult acting on behalf of a child and a library staff member who provides help with or knowledge, interpretation, or instruction, in the use of an information source.

Information sources include materials in all formats, as well as catalogs and other holdings records. Remember to include:

- Telephone, mail, and fax requests for information as well as in-person requests.
- Requests for help with the catalog, but not mechanical questions. (Count "How do I find books about the Holocaust in this catalog?" Do

not count "How do I turn this machine on?")
- Questions of fact. ("How long do flies live?")
- Requests for help in finding facts. ("How can I find out how long flies live?")
- General or specific requests for something to read. ("Can you help me find a good scary book?" "Is there another book as good as *Charlotte's Web?*")
- Requests for information and referral. ("Where can I take a puppy training class?" "Are there any clubs for baseball card collectors?")
- Data base searches.
- Requests by adults on behalf of children. ("I need a book about dinosaurs for my son." "Do you have any picture books I can read to my toddler that will help with potty training?" "Do you have books about Kwanzaa that I can read to my fourth grade class?")

Children's information transactions do not include:

- Directional questions. ("Where are the copy machines?")
- Questions about rules and policies. ("Is my two-year-old eligible for a library card?")
- Questions about library programs. ("Do you have a preschool story hour?")

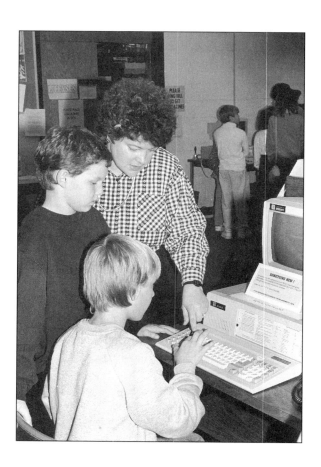

Children's Information Transaction Completion Rate

Definition: Percentage of information transactions by persons age 14 and under or by adults acting on their behalf that are completed successfully on the same day that the question is asked, in the judgment of the librarian.

Calculation: Divide NUMBER OF CHILDREN'S INFORMATION TRANSACTIONS COMPLETED by the total NUMBER OF CHILDREN'S INFORMATION TRANSACTIONS.

Data Collection: Reference staff tallies information transactions during two one-week sample periods, one in summer and one during the school year.

Example: During a typical week in summer, library users age 14 and under and adults acting on their behalf asked a total of 115 questions at both the children's and adult reference desks. Of these questions, 11 were directional questions and not counted as information transactions. Twelve questions were redirected to other departments or libraries. Eight questions were not answered or completed on the same day they were asked. Eighty-four questions were answered on the day they were asked; this is the Number of Children's Summer Information Transactions Completed. Subtract the number of directional questions (11) from the total number of questions asked (115) to find the Number of Children's Summer Information Transactions; the answer is 104. To calculate the Children's Summer Information Transaction Completion Rate, divide the Number of Children's Summer Information Transactions Completed (84) by the Number of Children's Summer Information Transactions (104); the result is .81, or 81 percent.

During a typical week during the school year, 156 questions were asked by people age 14 and under or by adults acting on their behalf. Sixteen were directional questions. Fifteen questions were redirected to other departments or libraries. Twenty questions were not answered on the same day they were asked. One hundred five questions were answered; this is the Number of Children's School Year Information Transactions Completed. Subtract the number of directional questions (16) from the total number of questions asked (156) to find the Number of Children's School Year Information Transactions (140). To calculate the School Year Information Transaction Completion Rate, divide the Number of Children's School Year Information Transactions Completed (105) by the Number of Children's School Year Information Transactions (140); the answer is .75, or 75 percent.

To calculate the annual **Children's Information Transaction Completion Rate**, convert the Summer Information Transaction Completion Rate and the School Year Information Transaction Completion Rate to decimals. Multiply the School Year Information Transaction Completion Rate (.75) by 3 to get a weighted average (2.25). Add the weighted school year average and the Summer Information Transaction Completion Rate (.81); the total is 3.06. Divide by 4 to get the **Children's Information Transaction Completion Rate** of .77, or 77 percent. There is a 77 percent chance that a child's information transaction (or that of an adult acting on behalf of a child) will be successfully completed on the day that it is asked.

$$\frac{84}{104} = .81 \qquad \frac{105}{140} = .75 \qquad \frac{.81 + (3 \times .75)}{4} = .77$$

Children's Information Transactions per Child

Definition:	Number of information transactions by persons age 14 and under or adults acting on their behalf per person age 14 and under in the community served.
Calculation:	Divide the ANNUAL NUMBER OF CHILDREN'S INFORMATION TRANSACTIONS by the CHILDREN'S POPULATION OF LEGAL SERVICE AREA.
Data Collection:	Library staff calculates questions during two one-week sample periods, one in summer and one during the school year.
Example:	During a typical week in summer, 145 information transactions were initiated by library users who were age 14 and under and by adults acting on behalf of children. Multiply 145 by 12 to get the Summer Children's Information Transactions (1740). During a typical sample week during the school year, 212 information transactions were initiated by persons age 14 and under. Multiply 212 by 40 to get the School Year Children's Information Transactions (8480). Add the Summer Children's Information Transactions (1740) and the School Year Children's Information Transactions (8480) to get the ANNUAL NUMBER OF CHILDREN'S INFORMATION TRANSACTIONS (10,220). In this community, the CHILDREN'S POPULATION OF LEGAL SERVICE AREA is 2450. To find the **Children's Information Transactions per Child**, divide the ANNUAL NUMBER OF CHILDREN'S INFORMATION TRANSACTIONS (10,220) by the CHILDREN'S POPULATION OF LEGAL SERVICE AREA (2450); the measure is 4.17. On average, children in this community and adults acting on their behalf conduct 4.17 information transactions during the year.

$$\frac{(145 \times 12) + (212 \times 40)}{2450} = 4.17$$

Note that these two measures are treated together because the same data collection methods are used for each; only the computation is different.

Collecting the Data

1. Select a typical week(s) to collect your data.
2. If, after tallying reference transactions for one week, you have not counted at least 100 separate transactions, keep counting for one more week. You need to have at least 100 transactions for the sample size to be meaningful.
3. You may collect data for the **Children's Information Transaction Completion Rate** at the same time as you collect data for the **Children's Information Transactions per Child** measure.
4. During the sample period, have staff at all service points record all information transactions initiated by library users who are age 14 and under and by adults acting on their behalf on the Children's Information Transaction Tally Sheet (Form 13). They should count at all times during the week, not just in selected periods. Number all tally sheets before you distribute them so you'll be sure to get them all back.
5. The Children's Information Transaction Tally Sheet includes a summary of directions for staff, but they may still get confused about what kind of question to record in what space. They may also be uncertain about how to distinguish a 14-year-old library user from a 15-year-old library user. Cover these issues in your staff training and plan to have a dry run for a few days before the sample week begins.
6. Remind staff that multiple questions from a single patron get multiple hash marks on the tally form.
7. Many times a parent accompanies a child to the library and speaks on behalf of the child or comes in alone to get materials for the child. Teachers also request help in getting materials that are then used by groups of children. These transactions should be recorded as children's information transactions because children are the end users of the materials.

Calculating the Measures

1. To calculate **Children's Information Transactions per Child** using two sample weeks, one

in summer and one during the school year, collect data as described for a typical week in summer and a typical week during the school year. Multiply the Number of Children's Information Transactions from the summer week by 12 to get the Number of Summer Children's Information Transactions. Multiply the Number of Children's Information Transactions from the school year week by 40 to get the Number of School Year Children's Information Transactions. Add the Number of Summer Children's Information Transactions to the Number of School Year Children's Information Transactions to get the ANNUAL NUMBER OF CHILDREN'S INFORMATION TRANSACTIONS. Divide the ANNUAL NUMBER OF CHILDREN'S INFORMATION TRANSACTIONS by the CHILDREN'S POPULATION OF LEGAL SERVICE AREA to determine **Children's Information Transactions per Child.**

2. To calculate **Children's Information Transaction Completion Rate**, collect data for a typical week in summer and a typical week in winter as described. For each week, tally the number of directional questions, the number of questions redirected, the number of questions not answered, the number of questions answered (NUMBER OF CHILDREN'S INFORMATION TRANSACTIONS COMPLETED), and the total number of questions asked. Subtract the directional questions from the total number of questions asked to get the NUMBER OF CHILDREN'S INFORMATION TRANSACTIONS. Divide the NUMBER OF CHILDREN'S INFORMATION TRANSACTIONS COMPLETED by the NUMBER OF CHILDREN'S INFORMATION TRANSACTIONS to get the Children's Information Transaction Completion Rate for each week. (The rate will be expressed as a decimal or as a percentage.) Multiply the School Year Information Transaction Completion Rate by 3 to get a weighted average. Add the weighted average to the Summer Children's Information Transaction Completion Rate and divide by 4 to get the annual **Children's Information Transaction Completion Rate.**

Interpreting and Using the Data

1. **Children's Information Transactions per Child** tells you the average number of questions asked by children or adults acting on their behalf for each child living in the Legal Service Area of the library. **Children's Information Transaction Completion Rate** tells you the percentage of informational or readers'

advisory questions asked by children age 14 and under or by adults acting on their behalf that are answered.

2. A high **Children's Information Transactions per Child** indicates high reliance on staff for assistance. This may mean that the staff is friendly and approachable or that the library has been successful in attracting large numbers of users of its juvenile collection. On the other hand, it may indicate that the library is particularly difficult to use or that large numbers of users lack basic library skills.

3. A low **Children's Information Transactions per Child** may indicate that the library is used primarily for borrowing materials, particularly if **Circulation of Children's Materials per Child** is high. (This would be appropriate for a library whose primary role is Popular Materials Center.)

4. A low **Children's Information Transactions per Child** combined with a low **Circulation of Children's Materials per Child** may indicate a low overall level of library use in the community. (On the other hand, if the library's primary role is Community Activities Center, and the programming measures are high, this result may be appropriate.)

5. A high **Children's Information Transactions per Child** combined with a low **Children's Information Transaction Completion Rate** may indicate either an emphasis on speed and volume rather than thoroughness or a small collection. A branch may have a low **Children's Information Transaction Completion Rate** because it is referring reference transactions to the central library.

6. A high **Children's Information Transaction Completion Rate** combined with a low **Children's Information Transactions per Child** may indicate that the emphasis is on serving a few people well or concentrating on a certain kind of question.

7. If you want to increase the **Children's Information Transactions per Child,** consider these ideas:

   • Publicize the kinds of reference and readers' advisory assistance that you are able to provide.
   • Increase the visibility of the service desk where children's reference transactions are handled.
   • Be sure that all staff members are trained to handle children's reference transactions.
   • Be sure that young people feel comfortable asking for help at all service points.

- Encourage staff to *offer* assistance with the use of children's materials rather than wait to be asked.
- Increase staffing at reference desks.

8. If you want to decrease **Children's Information Transactions per Child**, you could try the following:

- Make the library easier to use by rearranging the collection, improving access to the catalog, or improving the signage.
- Offer bibliographic instruction to help users of the children's collection become more independent.

9. If you want to increase the **Children's Information Transaction Completion Rate**:

- Offer staff development aimed at more effective information service to children; don't forget to train the adult reference staff as well as the children's staff.
- Increase staffing at reference desks.
- Analyze the collection to see if there are areas that should be improved.

Further Possibilities

1. On the Children's Information Transaction Tally Sheet (Form 13), divide each space for hash marks into two sections, one for adult clients and one for children (age 14 and under). This is particularly helpful when there is a Children's Service Desk that is staffed at all times; it gives you a feel for the use of the children's materials by both adults and young

people. You could calculate the Number of Children's Information Transactions by Adults and the Number of Children's Information Transactions by Children.

2. Record questions by time and day; then analyze to determine the periods of heaviest reference work load.

Programming

Most public library service plans include some provisions for programming. This section suggests some ways to measure and quantify programs that are conducted as part of the library's overall plan of service to children. The approach is similar to that taken for programming in *Output Measures for Public Libraries,* second edition.

A program is defined here as any planned event that introduces library services, provides information or entertainment, or promotes the library. It may take place in the library or elsewhere in the community, but the library must be a primary sponsor of the event, contributing time, money, space, or people to the planning or presentation of the program.

The basic program measured in this section is the program for which the primary intended audience is children—a puppet show, story hour, film program, magic show. Include in this measure programs for special groups, such as tours for Scout troops. Programs conducted for school groups, however, such as book talks for classes visiting the library, are accounted for in the following section, Community Relations.

Children's Program Attendance per Child

Definition:	Attendance by all ages at children's programs per person age 14 and under in the population served.
Calculation:	ANNUAL CHILDREN'S PROGRAM ATTENDANCE divided by the CHILDREN'S POPULATION OF LEGAL SERVICE AREA.
Data Collection:	Count the audience at all programs for which the primary audience is children during the entire year.
Example:	In one library, 3617 people attended children's programs at the library throughout the year. There are 1512 children age 14 and under in the community. The **Children's Program Attendance per Child** is 2.3. On average, each child in the community attended 2.3 children's programs at the library during the year.

$$\frac{3617}{1512} = 2.3$$

Collecting the Data

1. Use an actual count of all people attending children's programs to determine the ANNUAL CHILDREN'S PROGRAM ATTENDANCE. Programming varies too much over time to be captured accurately in a sample period.
2. Count adults as well as children who attend programs intended primarily for children.
3. If your library doesn't already have a way of keeping track of program attendance, you may want to use a Children's Programming Log (Form 14), such as the one we have provided in the Appendix.

Interpreting and Using the Data

1. This measure accounts only for the volume of attendance at each children's program conducted under the sponsorship of the library. It does not measure satisfaction with those programs, nor does it indicate the impact of the programs. You could use qualitative measures, such as focus groups or surveys, to understand the more subjective indicators that frequently interest decision makers or funding agents.
2. ANNUAL CHILDREN'S PROGRAM ATTENDANCE does not indicate how many of the total attendees are repeaters. In the example given, you cannot really claim that every child in town attended at least two programs. It is possible that a relatively small number of children account for a large part of your program attendance. However, the measure does give you a consistent way to compare your total program attendance with the number of children in your service area and provides a standard reference point that you can compare over time. It gives a meaningful indication of the level of service provided. The unit of analysis is attendance, not attendees. If it becomes very important to know how many individual children attend programs, you could ask children to sign in or register at each program and keep a separate log by name. This requires a level of effort, however, that most libraries could not and need not maintain.
3. If you want to increase **Children's Program Attendance per Child,** you might:

   - Have more programs.
   - Publicize programs more effectively.
   - Repeat successful programs.
   - Offer programs that can be attended by larger groups.
   - Evaluate the kind of programs you are offering.
   - Target particular groups of children, e.g., preschoolers, middle grade boys, latchkey children.
   - Cosponsor programs with other community groups.

4. Note that in some cases high program attendance may not be desirable. Many programs for preschoolers are more effective if the audience is fairly small and intimate, perhaps under 25. (Most Children's Librarians would want even smaller groups at toddler story hours.) A book discussion group for middle school children would be more meaningful for 10 participants than for 50 participants. A program featuring a popular children's entertainer or author may draw such a large crowd that it is difficult for anyone to enjoy the event. This output measure, therefore, is one that requires some caution in evaluating.

Further Possibilities

1. Calculate the annual and average attendance per juvenile program. Report by kind of pro-

gram, such as preschool story hour, computer club, martial arts demonstrations.

2. For the Summer Reading Program, calculate the Summer Reading Program Participation per School Age Population.

3. Calculate Preschool Story Hour Attendance per Preschool Child.

4. Keep a separate count of annual and/or average attendance at family programs. It may be useful to relate this to numbers of households in your community. Demographic sources, such as *Donnelly Demographics,* can provide the number of households.

5. Keep a separate count of annual and/or average attendance by adults at programs for adults conducted by the Children's Librarian, such as parenting programs or talks about children's books.

6. Relate program attendance figures to other measures, such as **Building Use by Children, In-Library Use of Children's Materials per Child,** or **Circulation of Children's Materials per Child.** This could be particularly useful if segmented to show library use by a particular part of the population, such as preschoolers, compared to other possible users. You might discover, for example, that **Picture Book Circulation per Child** and **Preschool Story Hour Attendance per Preschool Child** are much higher than the more general **Circulation of Children's Materials per Child** or **Children's Program Attendance per Child.**

Community Relations

This section provides techniques for measuring various activities involving the library and other community institutions or groups. This is a new category of output measure; it was not included in *Output Measures for Public Libraries,* second edition. We present this category because library services for children typically involve active working relationships with schools, child care centers, and other community organizations and agencies that serve children and youth.

- **Class Visit Rate** measures visits of school classes to the library.
- **Child Care Center Contact Rate** deals with contacts between the library and child care centers in the community.
- **Annual Number of Community Contacts** counts contacts between the library and other community groups, agencies, and organizations.

Because these are new output measures and because by their nature they deal with data that will vary considerably from community to community, the definitions are more flexible than those of the other measures. Implementing these output measures may not yield the same standardized results as the other measures presented in this manual. However, if you are consistent about how you define what you are counting and about how you collect your data, you will be able to compare results over time in your own library.

Class Visit Rate

Definition:	The number of visits by school classes to the library relative to the number of school classes in the community.
Calculation:	ANNUAL NUMBER OF CLASS VISITS TO THE LIBRARY divided by NUMBER OF CLASSES IN THE LEGAL SERVICE AREA.
Data Collection:	Count all class visits to the library. Take a census of the number of elementary, middle school, and junior high classes in the community.
Example:	In one library, 34 classes visited the library during the year. A census of elementary and junior high schools in the community showed that there are 2 elementary schools with 14 classes at each school, 1 junior high with 25 homeroom classrooms, and 1 parochial school with 8 classes. The NUMBER OF CLASSES IN THE LEGAL SERVICE AREA is 61. The **Class Visit Rate** is .55. If each class visited just once, 55 percent of the school classes in the community visited the library during one year.

$$\frac{34}{61} = .55$$

Collecting the Data and Calculating the Measure

1. Keep a log of all classes that visit the library for any purpose—book talks, library orientation, story hours, and so forth. If you don't already have a way to keep track of class visits, you may want to use the Class Visit Log (Form 15) that we have provided in the Appendix. The total number of classes visiting the library is the ANNUAL NUMBER OF CLASS VISITS TO THE LIBRARY.

2. Take a census of the number of classes in your Legal Service Area. Contact each school and ask for the number of grades and number of classes per grade. In schools with homerooms, ask for the number of grades and the number of homerooms. If you don't already have a way to keep track of this kind of school information, you may want to use forms similar to the School Survey Form (Form 16) and School Survey Summary (Form 17) that we have provided. The total number of classrooms serving children age 5 to 14 is the NUMBER OF CLASSES IN THE LEGAL

SERVICE AREA. In addition to providing data for the **Class Visit Rate**, this information will help you understand the demographics in your community and help you plan your overall program of library service to children.

3. To find the **Class Visit Rate**, divide the ANNUAL NUMBER OF CLASS VISITS TO THE LIBRARY by the NUMBER OF CLASSES IN THE LEGAL SERVICE AREA. The number may be smaller or greater than 1.0.

Interpreting and Using the Data

1. Note that the measure does not indicate whether the ANNUAL NUMBER OF CLASS VISITS TO THE LIBRARY consists of repeating classes. When the **Class Visit Rate** is more than 1.0, it certainly indicates that at least one class has visited the library more than once.

2. Objectives for **Class Visit Rate** will vary among libraries. If your policy is to invite each class in the community to visit the library once for an orientation to its services, then your objective might be to have a **Class Visit Rate** of 1.0, indicating that each class

had indeed visited the library one time. If your library has decided to be a Formal Education Support Center, you may be aiming for an active schedule of regular visits from many classes and a higher **Class Visit Rate**. If your library is trying to emphasize after-school activities or some other aspect of your service plan, you may prefer a lower **Class Visit Rate**.

3. Whatever your objectives, the **Class Visit Rate** is an indicator of the use of the public library by another public institution and may be

interesting to elected officials, parents, and other stakeholders in the community.

Further Possibilities

1. Take a census of preschool classes in your community and keep a log of the number of visits by preschool classes to the library. Calculate a Preschool Class Visit Rate.

2. Keep track of the number of visits the librarian makes to local elementary, middle, and junior high schools. Calculate a School Visit Rate (number of school visits divided by the number of schools in the Legal Service Area).

Child Care Center Contact Rate

Definition:	The number of contacts between the library and child care centers relative to the number of child care centers in the community.
Calculation:	ANNUAL NUMBER OF CHILD CARE CENTER CONTACTS divided by NUMBER OF CHILD CARE CENTERS IN LEGAL SERVICE AREA.
Data Collection:	Count all contacts between the library and child care centers. Take a census of the number of child care centers in the community.
Example:	In one library, the Children's Librarian visited each of the 5 child care centers in her community once during the year to introduce herself and the services the library could provide. In addition, 2 of the child care centers made a total of 9 visits to the library for story hours. The ANNUAL NUMBER OF CHILD CARE CENTER CONTACTS is 14. The NUMBER OF CHILD CARE CENTERS IN LEGAL SERVICE AREA is 5. Divide the ANNUAL NUMBER OF CHILD CARE CENTER CONTACTS by the NUMBER OF CHILD CARE CENTERS IN LEGAL SERVICE AREA to find the **Child Care Center Contact Rate** (2.8). On average, each child care center had 2.8 contacts with the library during the year. $$\frac{14}{5} = 2.8$$

Collecting the Data and Calculating the Measure

1. A *contact,* for the purpose of this measure, is any visit made by a library staff person to a child care center for any purpose or any visit made by groups from the child care center to the library.

2. Keep a log of all visits made to child care centers and all visits made by child care center groups to the library. If you don't already have forms that provide this information, you may want to use the Child Care Center Contact Log (Form 18) that we have provided in the Appendix. The total number of child care

center contacts in a given year is the ANNUAL NUMBER OF CHILD CARE CENTER CONTACTS.

3. Take a census of the number of child care centers in your Legal Service Area. You will need to define child care centers in the context of your own community. In some situations, only institutional child care centers would be counted. In other communities, you might want to also include licensed home day care providers. The total number of day care centers is the NUMBER OF CHILD CARE CENTERS IN LEGAL SERVICE AREA.

4. Divide the ANNUAL NUMBER OF CHILD CARE CENTER CONTACTS by the NUMBER

OF CHILD CARE CENTERS IN LEGAL SERVICE AREA to find the **Child Care Center Contact Rate**. The number may be more or less than 1.0.

Interpreting and Using the Data

1. As with the **Class Visit Rate**, different libraries will have different objectives and different interpretations of their **Child Care Center Contact Rates**. Libraries that are trying to keep a high profile in the community or that have chosen such roles as Community Activities Center or Community Information Center may want to achieve high **Child Care Center Contact Rates**. Other libraries may want to calculate this measure just to see how their service to day care centers compares with service to other institutions or with more general programs for children. In communities where few children are enrolled in child care, this may not be a meaningful measure.

2. Note that the measure does not indicate whether the ANNUAL NUMBER OF CHILD CARE CENTER CONTACTS are repeat contacts. It is possible that one nearby center will be responsible for a large number of the contacts while other centers have no contact with the library at all. The measure itself will not tell you anything about the pattern of the contacts. The log, however, will provide you with information about the pattern.

3. Like the **Class Visit Rate**, the **Child Care Center Contact Rate** is an indicator of library involvement with other community institutions and may be of particular interest to elected officials, parents, and other stakeholders.

4. This measure will be particularly important if your library has chosen Preschoolers' Door to Learning as a role. You will want to know which centers offer care to preschoolers.

Annual Number of Community Contacts

Definition:	Annual number of community contacts made by library staff responsible for service to children.
Calculation:	Count number of community contacts.
Data Collection:	Keep a record of all community contacts made by library staff responsible for service to children.
Example:	During the course of the year, the Children's Librarian prepared 12 press releases (which were published), attended 4 meetings of the Child Care Coalition and 2 meetings of the PTA, met twice with a community social worker, went 4 times to the local well-baby clinic to talk to staff and leave flyers about Family Story Time, visited each of the 3 recreation centers in the community, and spoke once for the Rotary Club. The **Annual Number of Community Contacts** is 28. The Children's Librarian made 28 contacts with the community during the year.
	$$12 + 4 + 2 + 2 + 4 + 3 + 1 = 28$$

Collecting, Calculating, Interpreting, and Using the Data

1. Keep a log of all community contacts. For the purpose of this measure, a community contact is any contact with the community made on behalf of library service to children. The contact may be with a community leader, an organization, an institution, or the media. Count visits to schools only if you are *not* keeping a separate School Visit Rate. Count only face-to-face contacts, not telephone calls. Count each press release that is published as a community contact. If your library has no way of keeping track of community contacts, you may want to consider using the Community Contact Log (Form 19) that we have provided in the Appendix.

2. This measure is expressed as a raw number, not as a ratio. It is probably most useful as a

simple quantification of the community contacts made by the Children's Librarian. It can be a work load indicator as well as an indicator of the level of effort made by Children's Services staff in a particular library to make contact with the community. It can be used to compare the number of community contacts made in different years or throughout different periods during the year.

3. The Community Contact Log can serve as a useful directory to individuals, organizations, and groups in the community that are involved with children. New Children's Librarians can analyze previous logs as one way to begin understanding a community.

Other Measurement Techniques

This final section deals with measures and measurement techniques other than the standardized output measures for public libraries. We include them because we feel they add richness to the standardized output data.

Some of the techniques described in this section are called *qualitative* to distinguish them from data collection techniques that focus on quantifying, or assigning numbers to things. These qualitative findings are designed to help you understand more subjective phenomena: thoughts, attitudes, feelings. Often the data that you acquire through qualitative methods help you understand or interpret the quantitative data you have acquired through other means. These qualitative methods are still empirical, that is, they still involve the collection of data from which conclusions and interpretations are drawn through analysis. It's just that the data yield more subjective findings.

The two data collection techniques that are discussed in this section are focus groups and user surveys.

Focus Groups

A focus group is a small number of people (usually 5 to 12) who discuss and give their opinions and ideas about a predetermined topic in response to questions from a facilitator. Focus groups were originally designed for social science research and then were adopted by advertising as a primary tool in market research. They have recently been rediscovered as a technique for applied research in many areas, particularly program evaluation.

When to Use a Focus Group

Focus groups are useful in many aspects of the applied research involved in measuring the output of your library service program:

- To help clarify issues before developing a quantitative research design.
- To help you interpret and understand the results of your quantitative output measures.
- To help you understand the attitudes or ideas of a target group of people.
- To help you evaluate current and/or prospective services, goods, or programs offered to a target group of people.
- To get information from children. Children are sometimes too shy or eager to please to provide valid information in a one-to-one interview, and they are often not competent enough to perform well on a paper-and-pencil questionnaire. The synergy of the group discussion seems to produce particularly good results with children.

Administering a Focus Group

1. Select participants for the focus group interviews.

   - Five to twelve people is the usual size for a focus group. If the participants are children, keep the number fairly small, no more than seven or eight. Children, especially very verbal kids, tend to get impatient waiting their turn to speak when the group is large. On the other hand, if you have fewer than five children, it is sometimes difficult to get a good discussion going.
   - The participants should represent a target population with some common characteristics, for example, single working mothers, Spanish-speaking library users, fourth grade students, or junior high school science teachers.

- Children age 9 years and older should do well in a half-hour focus group if it is well planned, with concrete questions that capture their interest. Younger children are a more unpredictable and unreliable target group; they need more encouragement to talk in a group and need *very* specific questions. Preschoolers are too young for focus groups that rely on verbal responses.
- It is best if the participants don't know each other well. For example, children from the same fourth grade class will be more involved with the dynamics of their own social relationships than with responses to your questions.
- You may need to have written approval from the parents when you are working with children. Check the policy in your library. See the sample Parent Consent Form (Form 20) in the Appendix. Form 20a is a Spanish translation of the Parent Consent Form.
- Explain *briefly* to the participants what you are researching and why you are doing it. For example, explain that you are trying to find out what library services working parents find most useful now and what library services they would like to see offered in the future.

2. Schedule focus groups.

   - Plan to conduct at least one trial focus group. This will enable you to pretest your questions and group process techniques.
   - Sometimes you need to conduct only one group. One group session may be enough to help you get a feel for the issues you want to explore in more depth or to help you interpret and understand findings of survey research.
   - If you need to feel more confident that the opinions and ideas you are hearing can be generalized to a greater population than the participants, you will need to conduct three to four groups with similar populations. The rule of thumb is that you can stop conducting focus groups on a particular subject when you are able to predict what the answers to your questions will be!
   - A typical focus group with children will be one-half hour to forty-five minutes long. Adult focus groups may last from forty-five minutes to an hour and a half.

3. Develop your questions.

   - You will usually ask about 5 questions, with possible follow-up queries for clarification.

- The questions should be open-ended but focused on the subject you want to know about.

  "Why do you take your child to the public library?"

  Not

  "Do you ever take your child to the public library for homework purposes?"

- Children tend to respond best to fairly concrete questions.

  "What problems do kids have trying to find what they want in the computer catalog?"

  Not

  "What problems do kids have using the library?"

- Here is a sample set of questions designed to find out what services working parents want from the library for their school-age children.

  a. What are the best services or programs that this public library provides for children and families?
  b. What problems do working parents have using the library with their children? Follow-up question: Can you think of any solutions to those problems that the library could try?
  c. What services or programs would you like to see the library provide for you and your children?
  d. Are there any agencies or organizations in this community that do a particularly good job providing service to children and families? What makes them so good?
  e. What should the public library's number one priority be?

- Here is a set of sample questions designed to find out what a group of 10-year-olds who participated in the Summer Reading Program thought about the experience:

  a. Why did you join the Summer Reading Club this year?
  b. What did you think of the theme?
  c. What did you think of the prizes?
  d. What did you think of the weekly programs?
  e. What was the worst thing about the Summer Reading Club?
  f. What was the best thing about the Summer Reading Club?

4. Conduct the focus group.

- Have the meeting in a comfortable, safe, or neutral location. Most participants like to sit around a table, but sometimes children feel more at ease on pillows on the floor.
- Have a tape recorder (with good batteries) and audiocassette plainly visible on the table.
- Explain again what you are doing and why. Be brief.
- Assure participants that what they say is confidential, that the tape will be used only to help you remember what was said, and that no one will be identified in any written report of the focus group. Tell them what will be done with their input, for example, it will be included in a report that goes to the Library Board. (Avoid promising any action as a result of their input.) Be brief.
- Explain that this isn't a test, that there are no right and wrong answers. Be clear that you

genuinely want to know what they think. Again, be brief. You want to listen to them.

- Keep note taking to a minimum. Concentrate your attention on listening and understanding what you are hearing. It is helpful to have a colleague present to listen and take notes.
- Encourage each person to respond to each question, but respect any person's desire to remain silent.
- Allow participants to respond to each other; sometimes you get the best insights from their interaction.
- Keep participants on the topic unless their digressions are potentially useful.
- Avoid giving your own opinions or judgments on what is said. Active listening techniques may encourage and clarify the discussion, however. Try occasionally repeating a participant's statement in slightly different words.
- When you have finished your prepared questions, ask if there are any last remarks that will help you understand what the participants have to say on this subject.
- Thank everybody for participating. Assure the participants that they have been helpful.
- Avoid promising the participants that they will see the results of the focus group unless you have already agreed to this as a condition of their participation.

Interpreting and Presenting the Results

1. Professional market researchers would have a typed transcript made of the focus group(s). This is a very labor-intensive process and is prohibitive for most libraries. Listen to the tape again as soon as possible after the focus group and make notes of major themes, issues, or concerns.
2. Write down the three or four major themes. These are your findings. Support each statement with several direct quotes from the taped discussion; this is your evidence. For example:

   A. Parents bring their children to the public library to do research for school reports.

   - "My son always waits until the last minute and *then* tells me he needs something from the library."
   - "I asked both kids why they don't do

this homework at the school library, and they both told me that the school library doesn't have enough books."
   - "Her teacher tells her she has to read one library book every month, and it has to be at the fourth grade level."

   B. Parents bring their children to the public library because they want them to be readers.

   - "I love to read, and I want Maria and Carlos to love reading, too."
   - "I didn't have libraries when I was growing up, and I know I missed a lot. I want my kids to have all the books they need."
   - "You can't get ahead if you don't read."

   C. Current service hours make it difficult for parents to bring their children to the public library.

   - "There's never any time during the week. By the time I get home from work and finish supper, the library is closed."
   - "Why isn't the library open on Sunday afternoon? That would be the best time for us to come. That's our family day."

3. If you need to make a formal written report, you can use the following sample outline as a guide.

What Working Parents Want from the Public Library: A Needs Assessment

1. Purpose of the study.
2. Study procedures.

   A. Describe focus groups (and any other methods you used to collect data).
   B. Be specific about the number of focus groups conducted, the nature of the target population, and the number of actual participants as well as the time frame in which the focus groups were held. For example, "Four focus groups were conducted with working parents who were recruited through the six elementary schools in the community. Twenty-two mothers and eight fathers participated in the focus groups that were conducted by Vivian Mitnick, Children's Librarian at the Eagle Rock Branch, and held at the library in November 1991."

3. Results. Use the format described in the section Interpreting and Presenting the Results on page 64.
4. Discussion. Elaborate on the implications of the results.
5. Recommendations.

User Surveys

User surveys are studies of people who use a library service. The usual intent of such surveys is to find out what the users think about the service or to rate their level of satisfaction with the service. Sometimes surveys are used to find out what new services people might be interested in. Simple user surveys are also involved in the data collection for fill rates, described in the section on Materials Availability Measures. There the effort was to get objective results through systematic sampling. In this section, we will deal with user surveys that try to get more specialized data from smaller groups of people.

Survey design is very difficult to do right. This section will only suggest some of the issues involved. Be sure to check the Sources for Additional Information at the end of Part 3 or other guides to survey research if you plan to seriously use surveys as a technique to measure library outputs or assess community needs.

When and Why

1. Sometimes the *only* way to get information from library users is to ask them for it.
2. Like focus groups, surveys can sometimes help you understand the results of quantitative data collection. For example, if your measurement effort shows that the Preschool Story Hour Attendance per Preschool Capita is decreasing and you can't figure out why, a survey of parents using the picture book collection might suggest some reasons.
3. Surveys can sometimes suggest the impact of a service on the users. The output measures tell you only numbers of users or uses; they don't tell you why parents bring children to preschool story hour or what the impact of story hour attendance is on either child or parent. It takes more sophisticated research than we are suggesting here to give scientifically valid answers to those questions, but even simple surveys can sometimes give you clues or indicators that will help you understand the more subjective aspects of library usage.
4. The output measures in this manual tend to measure specific kinds of library usage. User surveys can sometimes indicate more general or subjective phenomena, such as satisfaction with library services.
5. Specific and limited questionnaires can sometimes help you design services that better meet the needs of your target audiences. For example, a survey of school-age children about how they get to the library might indicate the need for more bike racks or the hiring of a crossing guard for after-school hours.

Administering a User Survey

1. Know what you want to find out. The least effective surveys are those that are fishing expeditions with no particular purpose.
2. Know what you are going to do with the results of the survey. It is very discouraging for staff to get involved in the effort of administering a questionnaire and never hear the results, much less see any action.
3. Be clear about the target group. Do you want to know what means of transportation are used by school-age children using your library? If so, you will have to think about sampling techniques to reach that audience. Or do you want to know if parents attending Toddler Story Time actually use the finger plays and parenting techniques that are presented there? This would indicate a more limited audience; you would be sure that each parent attending Toddler Story Time gets a questionnaire.
4. Design the questionnaire very thoughtfully. Consider the age of the potential respondent. Keep it simple. Ask for no extraneous information just because it might be interesting to know. Keep the questions clear and unambiguous. Think about how you are going to tabulate the responses. We have included two sample questionnaires—a Summer Reading Program Survey (Form 21) and a Preschool Story Hour Survey (Form 22) along with suggestions for implementing and analyzing them. We have also provided Spanish translations of each (Forms 21a and 22a). You will find the forms in the Appendix.
5. Administer a pretest to a small group before launching on a major survey effort. The pretest will help you spot any ambiguities or other problems in the questionnaire as well as

any unforeseen difficulties in the process itself.

6. Schedule the survey. You may routinely give an evaluation form to each person who attends any library program. (Be sure that you really tabulate and analyze the results if this is your practice.) You may want to conduct a general user satisfaction survey in the Children's Department during a typical week in summer and a typical week during the school year. If you intend to repeat the survey on a regular basis, be sure that you are consistent about the timing and procedures so that you can at least make an attempt to compare results.

7. As with all other measurement efforts, clear any survey approach with your administrators and inform staff members about what you're doing.

Interpreting and Using the Results

1. Keep in mind that unless you have been particularly attentive to sampling issues and survey design, your survey probably lacks the rigor to produce statistically valid, reliable, and comparable results. You should be wary about how you interpret the results, looking at them as *suggestive* rather than conclusive.

2. For any questionnaire, it is a good idea to calculate the response rate. This is the percentage of usable responses you receive from the questionnaires that were distributed. In general, the higher the response rate, the more likely the results are to be useful, assuming that the sample is unbiased and responses are not coerced.

3. As you tabulate responses, ignore incomplete or blank answers. Never assume that you know what a user meant. Ignore multiple answers to questions that are designed to have only one response. (If you get many unusable responses, it is possible that your survey form was poorly designed; a pretest will help detect this.)

4. The additional, miscellaneous comments that people make when filling out questionnaires are often very useful. It is usually a good idea to make a summary of these in addition to the tabulation of the data.

5. For most simple survey forms that you will be administering, it is usually enough to count the different responses to each question and calculate some simple percentages. For example, in 20 responses to the question "Does your child remember and repeat the rhymes and finger plays he or she hears in Preschool Story Hour?", 7 parents, or 35 percent, answered *always*; 12 parents, or 60 percent, answered *sometimes*; 2 parents, or 10 percent, answered *never;* and 1 parent, or 5 percent, answered *don't know.*

6. The results of your survey may be incorporated into commentary on output measures in any reporting that is done to the administration, to the public, or to elected officials. The library's annual report may include the results of output measures as indicators of the library's success in reaching its objectives. In the narrative section, you might quote some of the findings from a particular survey that helps to explain or enrich the quantitative data. For example, in discussing a Preschool Story Hour Attendance per Preschool Population figure of .10, you might want to point out: "Attendance at Preschool Story Hour is 10 percent of the total number of preschoolers in the community. Preschool Story Hours are designed to provide a quality learning experience in an intimate environment. Librarians hope that the young children who participate will go away from their story hour experience with some of the experiences and skills needed for reading readiness. Indeed, 85 percent of the parents whose children attend Preschool Story Hour report that their children remember and repeat the rhymes and finger plays that they have heard there."

7. Survey results are often very useful in evaluating current services and designing new ones. For example, if you learned from your Summer Reading Survey that 85 percent of the participants are also involved in summer school and other activities, you might want to think carefully about coordinating your own activities with other scheduled events in the community. You might even decide to limit formal programs and concentrate on readers' advisory and other individual reading motivation strategies.

The following section is an example of a survey that you might want to adapt for your own purposes or use as a model for other kinds of surveys.

Summer Reading Program Survey

This survey is designed to gather feedback from current participants in a Summer Reading Program. Its purpose is to help you evaluate the program's effectiveness in order to increase participa-

tion next year. Because the target respondents are children, the form is brief and simple. Even so, some of the younger children might need help with it.

Administering the Survey

1. Make enough copies of the Summer Reading Program Survey (Form 21) to give to each child who has registered with the Summer Reading Program. Your own Summer Reading Program Survey will certainly include different questions and possible responses to reflect your program; this is a sample only. We have included a Spanish-language translation of the survey form (Form 21a); you may need other languages in your community. See Appendix for both Forms 21 and 21a.
2. Distribute the survey to children immediately after the program is over or as each child completes his or her participation in the program. Try to hand the survey to each child individually, asking him or her to fill it out and return it to you. Explain that you want to know his or her opinion of the Summer Read-

ing Program so you can try to improve it and increase participation the following year. Be ready to help younger children fill out the form if necessary. Mail the form to children you don't see during this period; ask them to return it to the library before school starts in the fall. (Or include a stamped, addressed envelope.)
3. Libraries with massive Summer Reading Program registrations may want to sample their participants. One way to do this would be to mail a questionnaire to every tenth or twentieth child registered

Tabulating, Interpreting, and Using the Results

1. Discard any unusable responses. Calculate the response rate (number of usable questionnaires divided by the number of questionnaires distributed).
2. Tally responses to each question. If the number of total responses is relatively small (under 50), you may be able to use a blank questionnaire to tally responses. Otherwise,

you will want to make a tally sheet with enough room to tally responses to each question.

3. Calculate percentages where useful. For example, you might want to know what percentage of the participants were boys or what percentage of the participants were also enrolled in summer school.

4. You might want to calculate simple cross-tabulations. For example, you might want to know if the theme appealed more to boys than to girls. Then you would make separate tallies of question 7 for each gender. Other cross-tabulations are possible, but each one involves a separate tally and calculation.

5. Be cautious about making sweeping interpretations based on the survey alone. Some results may indicate only that you need to make further investigations in order to figure out what's going on. For example, if an overwhelming number of respondents indicated that they didn't like the Summer Reading theme, you know only that they didn't like the Summer Reading theme. You *don't* know if liking the Summer Reading theme is a factor that contributes to participation in the Summer Reading Program. (Focus groups might help you find out.)

6. Analysis of the demographic data (age and gender) as well as information about the child's participation in other activities may help you target next year's program more effectively. If most of the participants cluster in a tight age range, you can plan programs that are particularly appropriate for that age. A wide age range, on the other hand, may indicate a need for a variety of different kinds of programs.

7. Analysis of the responses to Question 5 may help you plan the promotion of the coming year's program more effectively. For example, if you made an effort to visit every class to talk up the program but very few children answered that "the librarian told my class about it," you might decide that this was not an effective promotional technique. If a large number of children answered that "my mother or father told me about it," perhaps press releases and other adult-oriented promotions are effective in your community.

Further Possibilities

1. Design a survey for children who did *not* participate in the Summer Reading Program.

2. Design a survey to elicit parent satisfaction with the Summer Reading Program.

Preschool Story Hour Survey

This section will present a sample method for obtaining a qualitative evaluation of preschool story hour from parents whose children attend.

Administering the Survey

1. Make enough copies of the Preschool Story Hour Survey (Form 22) for each parent or care giver who brings a child to preschool story hour. We have provided a Spanish-language translation (Form 22a). Both forms are in the Appendix. Consider what other languages you might need. Remember that parents may bring their children to a story hour presented in English even if they themselves speak another language.

2. If your preschool story hour is presented as a series with set registration, give a survey form to each parent or care giver at the last session. If your preschool story hour is a drop-in story hour with irregular attendees, ask parents to fill in a form at each story hour. Tell them they don't need to fill one in again if they have done so previously.

3. The Preschool Story Hour Survey form that we have provided is a basic one that incorporates many typical elements of preschool story hour. Feel free to leave out any questions that don't apply to your situation. Be cautious about adding questions; this is about as long as such a survey should be.

Tabulating, Interpreting, and Using the Results

1. Tabulate the results at the end of a preschool story hour series or at a logical point in a continuous story hour programming effort. This particular form is not designed to evaluate individual preschool story hours.

2. The answers to Question 5 can be cross-tabulated with answers to Question 1 about the age of the child. There is a considerable developmental difference between a typical 2-year-old and a typical 4-year-old. If both ages are attending story hour, it is possible that the content will not be appropriate to both. You may discover, for example, that most parents of 2-year-olds find the content always appropriate and that parents of 4-year-olds never or only sometimes find it appropriate. You might

decide as a result to have two or three sections of preschool story hour, segmented by age.

3. If you discover that the follow-up activity sheet is rarely used, you might decide to eliminate that aspect of the story hour or change its format and focus.

4. Record your data both as raw numbers and as percentages. For example, "Twenty-four parents filled out evaluation forms for preschool story hour. Twenty-two parents, or 92 percent, reported that they *always* check out books for their children when they come to story hour. Two parents (8 percent) said that they sometimes do."

Sources for Additional Information

Garbarino, James, et al. *What Children Can Tell Us: Eliciting, Interpreting, and Evaluating Information from Children*. San Francisco: Jossey-Bass, 1989.

A developmentally oriented guide to getting information from children.

Greenbaum, Thomas L. *The Practical Handbook and Guide to Focus Group Research*. Lexington, Mass.: Lexington Books, 1988.

Includes a good chapter on conducting focus groups with children.

Hutton, Bruce, and Suzanne Walters. "Focus Groups: Linkages to the Community." *Public Libraries* (Fall 1988): 149–52.

How focus groups were used in community analysis in one public library system.

Krueger, Richard A. *Focus Groups: A Practical Guide for Applied Research*. Newbury Park, Calif.: Sage Publications, 1988.

Using focus groups in applied research, which is what librarians do when they systematically study their user population or measure the outcomes of their service programs.

Leather, Deborah J. "How the Focus Group Technique Can Strengthen the Development of a Building Program." *Library Administration and Management* (Spring 1990): 92–95.

Basic focus group how-tos and how to apply them to a library building program.

Martyn, John, and F. Wilfrid Lancaster. *Investigative Methods in Library and Information Science: An Introduction*. Arlington, Va.: Information Resources Press, 1981.

Includes a useful chapter on questionnaire design.

Moran, Barbara B. "Construction of the Questionnaire in Survey Research." *Public Libraries* (Summer 1985): 75–76.

A good overview of the issues in questionnaire design.

Robbins, Jane, et al. *Evaluation Strategies and Techniques for Public Library Children's Services: A Sourcebook*. Madison, Wis.: University of Wisconsin–Madison, School of Library and Information Studies, 1990.

Includes a reprint of the Moran article and several examples of surveys designed especially for children's services.

Templeton, Jane Farley. *Focus Groups: A Guide for Marketing and Advertising Professionals*. Chicago: Probus Publishing Co., 1987.

A guide to the use of focus groups in market research.

Appendix: Blank Forms

FORM 1 Children's Library Visits Sampling Work Sheet

1. Total of all weekday morning visits made during the sample periods. (See Children's Library Visits Tally Sheet, Section A.)

(1) _____

2. Number of weekday morning hours in the sample periods (e.g., 3 hours Monday morning + 3 hours Wednesday morning = 6).

(2) _____

3. (1) divided by (2) = average number of weekday morning library visits per hour.

(3) _____

4. Number of weekday morning hours the library is open each week.

(4) _____

5. (4) × (3) = the estimated number of weekday morning visits per week.

(5) _____

6. Repeat steps 1–5 for (a) early afternoon, (b) after school, (c) evening, (d) Saturday, and (d) Sunday hours, and record the estimated number of (6a) weekday early afternoon, (6b) weekday after school, (6c) weekday evening, (6d) Saturday, and (6e) Sunday visits per week.

(6a) _____

(6b) _____

(6c) _____

(6d) _____

(6e) _____

7. (5) + (6a) + (6b) + (6c) + (6d) + (6e) = the estimated number of children's library visits each week.

(7) _____

8. Multiply (7) by 12 if this is a summer sample week. This is the estimated Summer Children's Library Visits count. If Summer Children's Library Visits count was taken earlier, record it in (8).

(8) _____

9. Multiply (7) by 40 if this is a school year sample week. This is the estimated School Year Children's Library Visits count. If School Year Children's Library Visits count was taken earlier, record it in (9).

(9) _____

10. Add (8) and (9) to get the estimated ANNUAL CHILDREN'S LIBRARY VISITS count.

(10) _____

11. Record CHILDREN'S POPULATION OF LEGAL SERVICE AREA.

(11) _____

12. Divide (10) by (11) to get **Children's Library Visits per Child**.

(12) _____

FORM 2   Children's Library Visits Tally Sheet

Date _____

Library/Entrance _____

Use one tally sheet each day per entrance. Enter number of hours during which data were collected. Count all individuals entering the library who appear to be 14 and younger, *including toddlers and babies.*

A. Morning Visits. Morning is from _____ a.m. to noon, or _____ hours.

Total morning visits _____

B. Early Afternoon Visits. Early afternoon is from noon to _____ p.m., or _____ hours.

Total early afternoon visits _____

C. After-School Visits. "After School" is from _____ to _____, or _____ hours.

Total after-school visits _____

D. Evening Visits. Evening is from _____ to _____ (closing time), or _____ hours.

Total evening visits _____

TOTAL VISITS THIS DAY _____

FORM 3 Building Use by Children Data Collection Form

_____ of _____

Library: _____ **Date:** _____

Directions: At sampling time, go quickly through the library and count the number of people age 14 and younger in each of the following spaces.

Spaces	Users										
	Time:	Time:	Time:	Time:	Time:	Time:	Time:	Time:	Time:	Time:	Time:
Total											

FORM 4 Furniture/Equipment Use by Children Data Collection Form

_____ of _____

Location or Department: _____   Date: _____

Directions: At sampling time, go quickly through the library and count the number of people age 14 and younger using each of the following:

Furniture/Equipment	Number Available	OBSERVATIONS											
		Time:		Time:		Time:		Time:		Time:		Time:	
		# in Use	Use Rate	# in Use	Use Rate	# in Use	Use Rate	# in Use	Use Rate	# in Use	Use Rate	# in Use	Use Rate

FORM 5 In-Library Use of Children's Materials Log

Area: _____

Date: _____

Use one tally sheet each day. Enter times at the top of the form. At each time listed on the log, collect and count the children's materials left for reshelving on tables, tops of shelves, floor, etc.

Type of Material	Time:	Time:	Time:	Time:	Time:	TOTAL
Nonfiction						
Picture Books						
Fiction						
Magazines						
Sound Recordings						
Other						
Other						
Other						
TOTAL						

FORM 6 Children's Materials Holdings Estimation Work Sheet

	Cards per inch	Vols. per inch
1. Take ten one-inch samples from the juvenile shelflist. For each sample count: a) cards per inch b) volumes or number of copies per inch	1a _____ 2a _____ 3a _____ 4a _____ 5a _____ 6a _____ 7a _____ 8a _____ 9a _____ 10a _____	1b _____ 2b _____ 3b _____ 4b _____ 5b _____ 6b _____ 7b _____ 8b _____ 9b _____ 10b _____

2. Compute totals of columns
   (a) and (b).   2c _____   2d _____

3. Divide (2d) by (2c) to get
   average number of volumes or
   copies per card.   3 _____

4. Measure the entire shelflist for Total
   Shelflist Inches.   4 _____

5. Divide (2c) by 10 to find Average Number of
   Cards per Inch.   5 _____

6. Multiply the Average Number of Cards per
   Inch (5) by the Total Shelflist Inches (4)
   to get Estimated Number of Cards in Shelflist   6 _____

7. Multiply the Average Number of Volumes per
   Card (3) by Estimated Number of Cards in
   Shelflist (6). Result is Estimated Number of
   Volumes in Shelflist.   7 _____

8. Enter number of items of children's materials not
   included in the shelflist.   8 _____

9. Add (7) + (8) for Total CHILDREN'S MATERIALS HOLDINGS. 9 _____

FORM 7   Children's Library Survey

Form # _____

1. How old are you? _____

    (If you are an adult looking for materials for a child, put down the child's age, not your own)

2. Were you looking for anything special in the library?   YES   NO

    Please tell us what you were looking for.

    1. _____

    Did you find it?   YES   NO   Was it for school?   YES   NO

    2. _____

    Did you find it?   YES   NO   Was it for school?   YES   NO

    3. _____

    Did you find it?   YES   NO   Was it for school?   YES   NO

3. If you were just browsing and not looking for anything special, did you find anything interesting?   YES   NO

4. Did you come to the library for some completely different reason, such as attending a program or using the restroom?   YES   NO

5. Is there anything else you want to tell us about the library? You may write on the back of the page if you want to.

Thank you for answering our questions. Please leave this form with the librarian today.

FORM 7a Cuestionario de la Biblioteca para Niños

Forma #_____

1. ¿Cuántos años tienes? _____

   (Si usted es un adulto buscando materiales para un/a niño(a), escriba la edad del niño(a), no la suya.)

2. ¿Estuviste buscando algo en particular en la biblioteca?

          Sí   No

   Por favor escriba lo que estuviste buscando.

   1. _____

      ¿Lo encontró? Sí No   ¿Era para la escuela? Sí No

   2. _____

      ¿Lo encontró? Sí No   ¿Era para la escuela? Sí No

   3. _____

      ¿Lo encontró? Sí No   ¿Era para la escuela? Sí No

3. ¿Si no estuviste buscando nada en particular, encontraste algo interesante?

          Sí   No

4. ¿Viniste a la biblioteca por algún diferente motivo, tal como para asistir un programa o ir al baño?

          Sí   No

5. ¿Hay algo más quisieras contarnos acerca de la biblioteca? Puedes escribir al otro lado de esta página.

Gracias por haber contestado nuestras preguntas. Por favor deja este cuestionario con el/la bibliotecario(a) hoy día.

FORM 8 Children's Library Survey Log

Form Number	(1) Title, subject, author				(2) Browsing		(3) Other	
	(a) Sought for school		(b) Not for school		(a) Browsers	(b) Found something	(a) Other	(b) Refused, blank, or missing
	(c) Found	(d) Not found	(e) Found	(f) Not found				
TOTAL								
	School items found	School items not found	Nonschool items found	Nonschool items not found	Number of browsers	Browsers finding something	Other	Not usable

FORM 9   Children's Library Survey Summary

1. Number of questionnaires handed out   _____

2. Questionnaires returned with usable title/subject/author or browsing answers
   (total of questions minus the total of columns 3a and 3b)   _____

3. Questionnaires with *only* "other" question checked (total of column 3a)   _____

4. Usable questionnaires (subtotal of lines 2 and 3)   _____

5. Questionnaires marked "refused," with no usable responses, or never
   returned (total of 3b)   _____

6. Response rate (line 4 divided by line 1)   _____

Children's Fill Rate

7. Title/subject/authors sought (total of columns 1c, d, e, and f)   _____

8. Title/subject/authors found (total of columns 1c and 1e)   _____

9. Title/subject/authors fill rate (line 8 divided by line 7)   _____

10. Number of browsers (total of column 2a)   _____

11. Number of browsers finding something (total of column 2b)   _____

12. Browsing fill rate (line 11 divided by line 10)   _____

13. **Children's Fill Rate** (total of line 8 and line 11 divided by total of
    line 7 and line 10)   _____

Homework Fill Rate

14. Title/subject/authors sought for school (total of column 1c and 1d)   _____

15. Title/subject/authors sought for school and found (total of column 1c)   _____

16. **Homework Fill Rate** (line 11 divided by line 12)   _____

FORM 10 Picture Book Use Survey

Form #_____

1. How old are you? _____

   (If you are an adult looking for materials for a child, put down the child's age, not your own.)

2. Were you looking for any particular picture books today?

   YES   NO

   What were they? Please tell us the name of the book you were looking for, or the author, of the subject.

   Did you find what you wanted? Please circle YES or NO for each item.

   1. _____

      Found?   YES   NO

   2. _____

      Found?   YES   NO

   3. _____

      Found?   YES   NO

3. If you were just browsing and not looking for anything special, did you find anything interesting?

   YES   NO

Thank you for answering our questions. Please leave this form with the librarian today.

FORM 10a Cuestionario del uso de libros con dibujos

Forma # _____

1. ¿Cuántos años tienes? _____

   (Si usted es un adulto buscando materiales para un/a niño(a), escriba la edad del niño(a), no la suya.)

2. ¿Estuviste bucando algún libro con dibujos hoy día?

   Sí   No

   ¿Cuales fueron? Por favor escriba el nombre del libro que estuviste buscando, o el autor, o el tema.

   ¿Encontraste lo que querías? Por favor pon un círculo alrededor de Sí o No por cada libro.

   1. _____

      ¿Fue encontrado?   Sí   No

   2. _____

      ¿Fue encontrado?   Sí   No

   3. _____

      ¿Fue encontrado?   Sí   No

3. ¿Si no estuviste buscando nada en particular, encontraste algo interesante?

   Sí   No

Gracias por haber contestado nuestras preguntas. Por favor deja este cuestionario con el/la bibliotecario(a) hoy día.

FORM 11 Picture Book Survey Log

Form Number	(1) Title, subject, author		(2) Browsing		(3) Other
	(a) Found	*(b)* Not found	*(a)* Browsers	*(b)* Found something	
TOTAL					
	Found	Not found	Number of browsers	Browsers finding something	Other

FORM 12   Picture Book Survey Summary

1. Number of questionnaires handed out _____

2. Total of column 3 ("other") _____

3. Questionnaires returned with usable title/subject/author or browsing answers (total number of questions minus the total of column 3) _____

4. Response rate (line 3 divided by line 1) _____

5. Title/subject/authors sought (total of columns 1a and 1b) _____

6. Title/subject/authors found (total of column 1b) _____

7. Title/subject/authors fill rate (line 6 divided by line 5) _____

8. Browsing materials sought (total of columns 2a and 2b) _____

9. Browsing materials found (total of column 2b) _____

10. Browsing fill rate (line 9 divided by line 8) _____

11. **Picture Book Fill Rate** (total of line 6 and line 9 divided by total of line 5 and line 8) _____

FORM 13 Children's Information Transaction Tally Sheet

Form # _____   Date _____

Library _____   Time period _____

Directions:

1. For each children's information transaction, put one hash mark (/) in section A, B, C, or D. Make one hash mark per transaction.
2. Count questions by users who are 14 and younger *or* by adults who are asking questions on behalf of young people, such as parents or teachers.
3. An information transaction is a contact which involves the knowledge, use, recommendations, interpretation, or instruction in the use of one or more information sources by a member of the library staff. Include information and referral transactions and requests by phone, mail, or fax as well as in person. Count readers' advisory contacts.
4. For users with multiple questions, record each question as a separate transaction if it deals with a new concern.

    A. Information Transactions Completed Today (user has received the requested information on the same day)

        Total A _____

    B. Information Transactions Redirected (e.g., to another department, library, or a nonlibrary source)

        Total B _____

    C. Information Transactions Not Completed Today (includes those completed at another time)

        Total C _____

    D. Other Questions (includes directional questions and other questions not included in the definition of reference transaction above)

        Total D _____

FORM 14 Children's Programming Log

Library _____

Month _____

Date	Name of Program	Number Attending
	TOTAL	

FORM 15 Class Visit Log

Library _____

Month _____

Date	Name of School	Grade	Teacher	Number Attending

Total Number Classes _____

Total Number of Students _____

FORM 16 School Survey Form

Library —————————————————

School —————————————————

    Principal ——————————————————————————————

    Other administrators ————————————————————————

    —————————————————————————————————

    —————————————————————————————————

    School Library Media Teacher ————————————————————

Grades covered ——————————————————————————

Number of classrooms —————————————————————————

Contact for parent organization ————————————————————

Reading scores ——————————————————————————

Comments:
(Note here any special services such as bilingual or special education classes, after-school
child care, etc.)

FORM 17 School Survey Summary

Library _____

Name of School	Number of Classrooms

Total Number of Schools _____

Total Number of Classrooms _____

FORM 18   Child Care Center Contact Log

Library _____

Month _____

Date	Child Care Center	Type of Contact	Number Attending

Total Number of Child Care Contacts _____

Total Number Attending _____

FORM 19 Community Contact Log

Library _____

Month _____

Date	Community Contact (name of organization, person, etc.)	Phone	Address

Total Number of Community Contacts _____

FORM 20   Parent Consent Form

I consent to allow my child _____

to participate in a focus group discussion that is being conducted by ___[researcher's name and organi-

zational affiliation]___ . I understand that this will be a group interview with five to seven children

answering questions about their library use. The group interview will last from 30 minutes to one hour

and will be held at ___[time]___ on ___[date]___ at ___[place]___ . The focus group interview will pro-

vide information that will help the public library staff evaluate the effectiveness of its current service to

children and design future programs.

I have been assured that sensitive topics will not be discussed and that my child will not be asked

to reveal any confidential information about himself or herself, his or her family, or his or her personal

life. I understand that every effort will be made to avoid making my child feel embarrassed or nervous

during the discussion and that my child may refuse to answer any question he or she may not wish to

answer.

I understand that my child will be audiotaped during the focus group. These tapes will be used only

to transcribe the discussion and analyze what was said. My child's identity will not be disclosed on the

tape or in any transcriptions that are made from the tape. The tapes will be destroyed as soon as the

study is completed.

If I have any questions, I will contact ___[name of responsible person]___ at ___[name of library]___

at ___[telephone number]___ .

I acknowledge that I have received a copy of this form.

_____   _____
Parent's signature   Date

FORM 20a   Declaración del Consentimiento del Padre o de la Madre

Declaración del Consentimiento del Padre o de la Madre

Yo permito que mi hijo(a) _____ participe en un grupo dirijida por [nombre del(a) investigadora(a) y su organización] . Yo comprendo que será una entrevista de un grupo de cinco a siete niños respondiendo preguntas acerca de sus usos de biblioteca. La entrevista durará entre 30 minutos a una hora empezando a las [hora] del [fecha] en [lugar] . La información que se conseguirá a consecuencia de la entrevista ayudará al personal de la biblioteca pública a evaluar la eficiencia de sus servicios actuales para niños y diseñar programas en el futuro.

Me han asegurado que no tocarán temas sensibles y que no le pedirán a mi hijo(a) información confidencial acerca de sí mismo(a), su familia or su vida privada. Yo entiendo que se hará todo esfuerzo posible para evitar que mi hijo(a) podrá negar a contestar cualquier pregunta que quiera.

Yo entiendo que van ha grabar la conversación durante la entrevista. Las cintas van a ser usadas sólamente para transcribir la conversación y analizar lo que transcurrió. La identidad de mi hijo(a) no va a ser indicada en la cinta o en las transcripciones. Las cintas serán destruidas una vez que termine la investigación.

Si tengo alguna pregunta, llamaré a [nombre de la persona encargada] en [nombre de la biblioteca] con el número de teléfono [número de teléfono] .

Yo declaro que he recibido una copia de esta forma.

_____   _____
Firma del padre o de la madre   Fecha

FORM 21 Summer Reading Program Survey

Please take a few minutes and answer these questions. Your answers will help us improve the Summer Reading Program next year!

1. How old are you? _____

2. Are you a boy or a girl? Circle the right answer. BOY GIRL

3. Make a check mark in front of any of these activities that you took part in this summer.

   _____ Summer school

   _____ Family vacation

   _____ Swimming lessons

   _____ Other lessons

   _____ Camp

4. How did you hear about the Summer Reading Program? Please check the right answer. You can check more than one answer.

   _____ My mother or father told me about it.

   _____ My teacher told me about it.

   _____ The librarian told my class about it.

   _____ I heard about it at the library.

   _____ Friends told me about it.

   _____ Some other way.

   _____ I don't remember.

More questions on the next page . . .

5. Make a check mark in front of the library activities that you took part in this summer. Draw a happy face after the activities that you especially enjoyed.

    _____ Reading books

    _____ Story hours

    _____ Awards ceremony

    _____ Magic show

    _____ Film programs

6. What did you think of the prizes this summer? Check the right answers. You can check more than one answer.

    _____ I didn't get any prizes.

    _____ Great!

    _____ Okay

    _____ Dumb

    _____ I don't care one way or the other.

7. What did you think of the theme of the Summer Reading Program this year? Check the right answer.

    _____ I didn't pay any attention to the theme.

    _____ I liked it.

    _____ I didn't like it.

    _____ I don't care one way or the other.

8. Tell us anything else you think we should know about the Summer Reading Program. You may write on the back of the page.

Thank you for answering our questions. Please give this form to the librarian today.

FORM 21a   Cuestionario del programa de lectura de verano

Por favor toma unos minutos para contestar las siguientes preguntas. Tus respuestas nos ayudarán a mejorar el programa de lectura de verano en el próximo año.

1. ¿Cuántos años tienes? _____

2. ¿Eres un niño o una niña? Pon un círculo alrededor de la respuesta correcta.

   Niño   Niña

3. Pon una marca al costado de las actividades en que participaste este verano.

   _____ Escuela de verano.

   _____ Vacaciones de familia.

   _____ Clases de natación.

   _____ Otro tipo de clases.

   _____ Campamento.

4. ¿Cómo te enteraste del programa de lectura de verano? Por favor marca la respuesta correcta. Tu puedes marcar más de una respuesta.

   _____ Mi madre o padre me lo dijo.

   _____ Mi maestro(a) me lo dijo.

   _____ El/la bibliotecario(a) se lo dijo a mi clase.

   _____ Me enteré de ello en la biblioteca.

   _____ Amigos me lo dijeron.

   _____ Me enteré de otra manera.

   _____ No me acuerdo

Más preguntas en la próxima página . .

5. Marque las actividades de la biblioteca en que participaste. Dibuja una cara sonriente al costado de las actividades que más te gustaron.

    _____ Leer libros.

    _____ Horas de cuento.

    _____ Ceremonia de premios.

    _____ Programa de magia.

    _____ Programas de pelicula.

6. ¿Qué te parecieron los premios de este verano? Marca las respuestas correctas. Tu puedes marcar mas de una respuesta.

    _____ No recibí ningún premio.

    _____ ¡Estupendo!

    _____ Bueno

    _____ Tonto

    _____ No me importa.

7. ¿Qué tal te pareció el tema del programa de lectura de este verano? Marca la respuesta correcta.

    _____ No me fijé del tema.

    _____ Me gustó.

    _____ No me gustó.

    _____ No me importa.

8. Cuéntanos cualquier otra cosa que necesitamos saber acerca del programa de lectura de verano. Puedes escribir al otro lado de esta página.

Gracias por haber contestado nuestras preguntas. Por favor entregue este forma a el/la bibliotecario(a) hoy día.

FORM 22 Preschool Story Hour Survey

Please take a few minutes to answer these questions. We are interested in knowing how you and the child you bring to the library respond to Preschool Story Hour.

1. How old is the child you bring to Preschool Story Hour? _____

2. Approximately how many times did you attend Preschool Story Hour this year? _____

3. Do you check out books for your child when you come to Preschool Story Hour? Circle the best answer.

   ALWAYS   NEVER   SOMETIMES   DON'T KNOW

4. Does your child remember and repeat the rhymes and finger plays that he or she hears at Preschool Story Hour? Circle the best answer.

   ALWAYS   NEVER   SOMETIMES   DON'T KNOW

5. Does the content of the Preschool Story Hour seem appropriate for your child? Circle the best answer.

   ALWAYS   NEVER   SOMETIMES   DON'T KNOW

6. Do you use the follow-up activity sheet with your child? Circle the best answer.

   ALWAYS   NEVER   SOMETIMES   DON'T KNOW

7. Would you recommend that a friend bring his or her child to Preschool Story Hour? Circle the best answer.

   YES   NO   MAYBE   DON'T KNOW

8. Is there anything else you'd like to tell us about your experience with Preschool Story Hour? Please feel free to use the back of the page.

Thank you for answering our questions. Please leave this form with the librarian today.

FORM 22a   Cuestionario de la hora de cuentos para niños preescolares

Por favor tome unos cuantos minutos para contestar estas preguntas. Nosotros estamos interesados en saber como usted y el/la niño(a) que usted trae a la biblioteca reaccionan a la hora de cuentos para niños preescolares.

1. ¿Cuántos años tiene el/la niño(a) que usted trae a la hora de cuentos? _____

2. ¿Aproximadamente cuántos veces han asistido a la hora de cuentos este año? _____

3. ¿Saca libros para su niño(a) cuando vienen a la hora de cuentos? Pon un círculo alrededor de la major respuesta.

      Siempre   Nunca   A veces   No sé

4. ¿El/la niño(a) se acuerda y repite las rimas y los juegos de dedos que el o ella escucha en la hora de cuentos?

      Siempre   Nunca   A veces   No sé

5. ¿Es el contenido de la hora de cuentos apropriado para su niño(a)?

      Siempre   Nunca   A veces   No sé

6. ¿Usa las hojas de actividades de proseguimiento con su niño(a)?

      Siempre   Nunca   A veces   No sé

7. ¿Recomendaría a un amigo(a) a que traiga a su niño(a) a la hora de cuentos?

      Sí   No   Quizás   No sé

8. ¿Hay algo que quisiera contarnos acerca de su experiencia con la hora de cuentos? Sientase libre de escribir en el otro lado de esta página.

Gracias por haber contestado nuestras preguntas. Por favor deja este cuestionario con el/la bibliotecario(a) hoy día.

Index

Virginia A. Walter is currently Assistant Professor at the Graduate School of Library and Information Science at the University of California at Los Angeles. Her M.L.S is from the University of California at Berkeley and her Ph.D. in Public Administration is from the University of Southern California. She teaches courses related to management, public library administration, and library service to children. Her research and writing deal primarily with the use of volunteers in public libraries, evaluation of public library services, and children's use of library and information resources.

Before joining the faculty at UCLA, Walter worked for more than twenty years in public libraries in California. She has been a Children's Librarian, Young Adult Librarian, Branch Library Manager, Regional Library Administrator, and Central Library Department Head. Most recently, she was the Children's Services Coordinator at Los Angeles Public Library.